The  Net

An Organizational Vision for the Church of Tomorrow

C.S.Wimmer

WESTBOW
PRESS
A DIVISION OF THOMAS NELSON
& ZONDERVAN

New Revised Standard Version Bible, copyright 1989, Division of Christian Education of the National
Council of the Churches of Christ in the United States of America. Used by permission. All rights reserved.

Author Credits: The poem, "When I say I am a Christian," copyright 1988

WestBow Press books may be ordered through booksellers or by contacting:

WestBow Press
A Division of Thomas Nelson & Zondervan
1663 Liberty Drive
Bloomington, IN 47403
www.westbowpress.com
1 (866) 928-1240

ISBN: 978-1-4908-4357-5 (sc)
ISBN: 978-1-4908-4356-8 (e)

Library of Congress Control Number: 2014912161

Printed in the United States of America.

WestBow Press rev. date: 08/05/2014

"The kingdom of heaven is like a net
that was thrown into the sea
and caught fish of every kind"

—Matthew 13:47

Contents

Preface

My journey of faith began in the deep end of the spiritual pool. I've never known anything different. Born to a mother who suffered with mental illness, my life was defined by abnormal responses to normal circumstances at an extremely young age. By the time I was seven years old, I was able to pronounce the words *paranoid schizophrenia* and explain exactly how this particular brain disease manifested itself in my personal world. Faith wasn't an option. It was a means of emotional and spiritual survival. God and I were a team from day one.

Oddly, however, I did not connect God with the church. In my childhood mind, the church was the red-brick building next to my elementary school. At some point in time, I learned that people sang songs in the building, which piqued my interest. Since I loved music, almost as much as I loved God, I asked to join the children's choir. From that point forward, the church became the place where God and I could sing together! That was its purpose—period.

Fast forward in time. As a young mother with two toddlers, I found myself directing children's music in a large church. Then, the opportunity to direct a youth choir came about, followed by a bell choir, theatrical events, a sacred dance group, a sewing ministry, and so on. From all outward appearances, I portrayed the epitome of spiritual fulfillment as twenty-two years flew by. But I wasn't entirely fulfilled. A gnawing existed deep within my soul that just wouldn't go away.

My relationship with God remained strong, yet my affiliation with the institutional church began to waver. Something wasn't right. I felt an incredible sense of call to disengage from traditional ministry and move on to something different. But that *something* was hidden from my heart until . . .

October 18, 1996

On this particular autumn day, my husband and I were driving through the Ozark Mountains on our way to the quaint community of Eureka Springs, Arkansas, USA. We had booked a Bed and Breakfast for a weekend get-away. Our plan was to stroll among the antique cars that were on display at the annual car show; do a little window shopping; enjoy our usual Italian dinner; then settle in for the night under the soft, down comforters at the Bed and Breakfast. It was an ordinary day that was about to turn extraordinary in the spiritual sense.

As we were driving, I thought about my personal journey: where I'd been and where I might be headed. Gazing out of the window at the beautiful autumn foliage, I thought to myself, "I am the church. The church lives in me. The church is not a place to which I take myself. I know, beyond a shadow of a doubt, that God has called me to remove myself from her institutional identity. I no longer fit her present model, but the separation feels like death to me . . . and I'm just plain sad—*really* sad!"

Then, in the midst of those private thoughts, something unexplainable happened. An image of vertical and horizontal lines, intersecting one another, appeared between my face and the windshield of our car. It looked like a grid of empty squares. The image entered my awareness with a simultaneous understanding of its purpose. Categories of ministry, such as: worship, education, evangelism, mission, etc., were positioned on the left side of the grid. The entire human lifecycle—infancy to elderly—spanned across the bottom of the grid from left to right. It formed an organizational foundation for comprehensive ministry that included all aspects of life and all age groups.

I reacted to the image with a silent gasp. "Oh, my goodness," I thought. "Why don't we [Christians] know about this? Why don't we *know* this?"

I'm certain I didn't blink as I stared at the empty space where a grid had become visible. I remained motionless long after the image disappeared—holding my breath while processing what had just happened. Time seemed to stop, in those few seconds, while a mixture of disbelief and reality hung in suspension. How does one react to an unexpected, *supernatural* interruption?!

Freezing in place seemed the natural thing to do.

Immediately, I sensed that the image of intersecting lines was connected to the *something more* that had been hidden from my heart. By the time we arrived in Eureka Springs, the inner gnawing that had been present within my soul for so many years, was strangely absent. Nothing changed outwardly, but the experience was so other worldly that I needed time to ponder the sudden change. So, I withheld those precious moments from my husband as we strolled among the antique cars. As planned, we did a little window shopping followed by a quiet, Italian dinner. Then we settled under the soft, down comforter at the Bed and Breakfast. In spite of feeling physically tired, my mind was wide-awake and whirling. Sleep was not an option.

March 20, 1997

Around midnight, I was aroused by the feeling of localized pressure on my chest, as if something—or *someone*—was standing on me. At first I thought I was experiencing the warnings of a heart attack, but the sensation only lasted for a few seconds. Then came the heat! Intense warmth radiated from the center of my heart outward to all parts of my body. I was hot from head to toe, but I didn't break a sweat. It was an internal form of heat that originated within my heart, yet never reached the outer realm of my flesh.

I could only wonder: *what is happening to me*? Yet, at the same time, I wasn't frightened. I felt completely calm. Then, I heard these words: *"Close the portals."* They were not spoken audibly. Instead, the words were expressed in a discernible but distinctly inexplicable way.

I reacted with internal surprise while numerous thoughts tumbled to the forefront of my mind. "Portals? *Seriously!* That's not a word I ever use. Who talks about portals? Not portholes—but *portals*! Do I even know the definition of this word?" Yes, I thought I knew the definition, but suddenly I wasn't confident in the preciseness of my memory.

Once again, sleep was not an option. I rolled out of bed and headed straight for my dictionary. The word *portal* is defined as a gateway, an entrance, or a wide opening! The word *porthole* is defined as a window in a boat or ship—usually round in shape. Thus, the command to close the portals was a command to close the gateways, entrances, and wide openings!

By March of '97, my mind had been opened to a deeper understanding of the grid that appeared between my face and the windshield of our car. I originally thought of it as a simple administrative tool for organizing ministry. However, as God's Spirit worked within me, I began to realize that the image was an organization of people—*a net*! Furthermore, the scriptural origin of *The Net* had also been slowly revealed.

As the depth of insight increased, I became troubled by the fact that the traditional church has not organized herself in accordance with the vertical and horizontal lines of *The Net*. Instead, she succumbed to humanity's default organizational image—the pyramid! She layered herself with differing levels of decision making in order to create a governmental institution. But the church never became a net. This fact opened my eyes to large vacancies in society where widespread netting is needed, but not currently present. Hence, the command to close the portals!

Many details remained a mystery to me that night, in March of '97. I couldn't help but ask: "What am I to do with this information?" I wish I could say that I felt empowered to go forth and close the portals, but in truth, I felt helpless and incompetent. I knew that the church's human attempts to organize God's people were less than optimal and I understood why the portals must be closed. But quite frankly, I felt intimidated by the command to close them! *"Why me*?!" I have a small voice and no authority. Who would listen even if I dared to speak?

October 18, 2000

Four years had passed since *The Net* appeared between my face and the windshield of our car. Due to a change in my husband's career, we had moved from Oklahoma, to the desert climate of Fresno, California. I mention this because I've come to think about my time in Fresno as my personal *desert experience*—spiritually unparalleled by anything previous, or anything since.

I came to realize that the vision of *The Net* was a precursor of things to come. From 1996 to 2000, repeated interruptions, of the supernatural kind, became almost *normal*. I grew accustomed to feeling hounded by the movement of God's Spirit within me—like a creature that is hunted down in hot pursuit! One insight after another would sometimes flow into my mind at breakneck speed. Then, everything would stop until I could process the insights. Once I could make sense of it, I found myself speeding ahead on the spiritual freeway, again.

In addition to *The Net*, God's Spirit revealed *The Key*—a visual language rooted in the images of Creation, as ordered in the text of Genesis 1. The language is common to all people, but seldom referred to when discussing spiritual matters. I also became aware of *The Clock*—a timekeeping method that also exists within the literary order of Genesis 1. While listening to *The Key* language of creation, and learning about time-related issues through *The Clock*, I felt like a kid in God's candy store. I couldn't believe the sweetness of the information—a pleasurable flavor I hadn't previously known, and haven't tasted since.

In total, God's Spirit filled me with exciting insights in three areas of human thought: time, language and organization. However, the massive amount of information came with a weighted sense of responsibility that was daunting! At one point I became so mentally fatigued that I yelled at God in exasperation: "You do realize that no one, repeat—*no one*—will ever believe me if I talk about these things! Where are we going with this, God? You know there is a history of mental illness in my family—visual and auditory hallucinations . . . objects that take on persecutory meanings! Why are you opening my eyes to this information? Is this a joke?"

No. I knew that the revealed knowledge wasn't a laughing matter. I was just stymied at that particular moment. The imparted insights were not bizarre or ridiculous. On the contrary—the information was logical, rational, and nourishing. The new knowledge led me to a deep place of spiritual healthiness and wholesome thinking. Yet, I was keenly aware that the knowledge was *extraordinary* and life altering!

The final supernatural interruption came on October 18, 2000—exactly four years after the initial vision of intersecting lines appeared between my eyes and the windshield of our car. I went to bed as usual and promptly fell into a deep sleep, but once again, I would not sleep through the night. This time, I was awakened around 3:30 a.m. to a jiggling sensation in my chest. It felt as though my heart was a glob of gelatin, quivering nervously on a plate, being carried by an elderly woman with feeble hands. Jiggle, jiggle—jiggle, jiggle. The sensation lasted for at least 15 to 20 seconds.

"Okay! Okay! I'm awake! Goodness!" I sighed, defenselessly. "What do you want of me? What am I supposed to do? I *don't know what you want me to do*!" Feeling helpless, yet again, I found myself in a state of mental transport. The vision that was placed before my mind, is described in the following paragraphs.

I was taken to a hillside where I sat in a forest of trees overlooking a valley floor. I faced north, while the valley stretched out before me in an east-west direction. The sun was high in the sky, but the trees provided a covering of shade for my body. I felt cool, relaxed, and peaceful, as I observed a sea of people standing out in the open valley.

I noticed that the people were enjoying each other's company. I also noticed that they meandered about in a directionless manner—just milling around while socializing. I remember feeling concern for them because of the heat. Since they had no protection from the hot, broiling sun, I was glad to be an observer rather than a participant.

Suddenly and silently the entire picture changed before my eyes. As if responding to a trumpet blast, or a call to order, the sea of people that had been aimlessly milling around, was now instantly organized in squares. Everyone faced west. As I watched from the hillside, the squares of people began to move—as if they had become one body responding to the beat of a drum that everyone could hear. But there was no sound!

Additionally, I noticed that no militancy or aggressiveness was present in the movement of the squares. In fact, the new order was a peaceful, pleasant movement of people—a beautiful sight to behold! As far as my eyes could see, the valley floor was covered with squares of people, like a quilt made of individual patches of fabric—different in appearance, but united in purpose.

As the square-shaped groups moved westward, I became aware of the fact that the sun no longer seemed hot. It simply provided light for the people in the valley. Then, as quickly as the vision began, it ended with a faint whisper: "The Lord's army marches 12 by 12."

That was that! All was silent. Once again, I was wide awake with thoughts that I'd never had before. In disbelief, I remember saying to myself, "I just *saw* the Lord's army!" I believed what I saw, but I couldn't believe I *saw* it! Unlike the first line of Sabine Baring-Gould's 1865 hymn, "Onward, Christian soldiers, marching as to war"— the Lord's army wasn't marching toward war in the traditional sense of combat. In fact, it wasn't marching at all! The people walked, quietly, calmly, and orderly, in an east-west direction—illuminated by light as it moved peacefully, yet intentionally.

February 3, 2014

Nearly eighteen years have come and gone since *The Net* appeared between my face and the windshield of our car. I've prayed about the command to close the portals, as well as the vision of a 12 by 12 *army* walking in squares. I've completed the necessary research in preparation for teaching the purpose of *The Net*. I've waited patiently for the right time to publish *The Net*, and then, let the Holy Spirit empower those who want to use it.

If I've discerned things accurately, a certain readiness for some type of new or different structure is slowly emerging. Those who have been called out of the traditional institution know that a continuation of the hierarchical systems of the church is not an option. Thus, I've heard spiritual leaders wonder about new organizational models—what they might look like and how they might function. After all, the mission of the church has not yet been completed. Failure is not an option—neither is quitting!

The good news is that the people of God *do not need to invent a new organizational model* for the church of tomorrow! A suitable model exists within the ancient words of the Bible. Our eyes simply need to be opened to the shape of a square! We need to *see* a net! Like textual archaeologists, we must unearth the image of *The Net* from the many layers of the scriptural tapestry. We must examine *The Net* and talk about its spiritual value. If we are willing to do this much, I am confident that future net makers will be born and portals will close.

Carol Wimmer

Introduction

These are not ordinary times. The spiritual air is swirling. Shifting winds are causing uncertainty and bewilderment, which can be both frightening and exciting. Some people ask, "Why can't things be the way they used to be?" Others whisper, "Thank God, things are changing!" To be certain, something is happening on a grand scale. As God's people in the Christian faith tradition, we have many things to ponder.

Will we fight against the spiritual gusts that push at us from differing directions, or will we allow our spirit to be carried to the place of God's desire? Time will tell. Hopefully, many souls will feel the presence of God's Spirit and submit without hesitation. For those who are willing to be carried along, God's guiding hand is sure to provide the best way to travel!

It is conceivable that this spiritual shift, perceived by so many people, is in its early stages with much stronger winds to come. The overall period of intense change could occur over many generations. In truth, significant transformations can take hundreds of years to complete. When all is said and done, however, I think history will look back on the present time and say, "God's Spirit intervened in a powerful way. Radical change occurred."

The church has undergone schisms and reformations in the past, but every previous change caused division among God's people. This time, the winds of change seem to be drawing God's people together—to listen, see, hear, and respond to different approaches in ministry; to discuss new ideas about what it means to be God's people;

and to listen to diverse perspectives regarding the ways that human beings honor God, etc. Hopefully the information in this book will contribute something of value to the present dialogue.

The material is presented in a modest manner with user-friendly language. The information is offered as seeds to be planted in the garden of human imagination. It is a simple *look* and *see* endeavor—written for spiritually minded people who (a) hold positions of leadership within the traditional church (b) have become disillusioned with the traditional church (c) feel called to envision something different for the church's future, or (d) sense a spiritual invitation to begin building the church of tomorrow.

The Net offers an organizational vision for the church of tomorrow. The main focus of the book is the study of a spiritually rooted structure, based on evidence found in the Bible. *The Net* is an egalitarian, shoulder to shoulder model that operates at a grassroots level. It contrasts hierarchical structures that employ different levels of decision making.

The Net is not affiliated with any particular vein in the present church body. Instead, it is a generic structure that is not attached to church doctrine, rituals, customs, or practices. Because *The Net* is generic in nature, I've chosen to address the traditional church from a universal perspective throughout this book. I speak of the church as the bride of Christ, because I believe that is her spiritual identity. Throughout the book, I employ female pronouns when referring to the church. I also suggest that, *to be properly dressed*, the bride of Christ must change her worldly appearance.

When contrasting *The Net* with the structure of the institutional church, I take a respectful, yet critical view, of the church's present image. In doing so, I fully acknowledge the fact that millions of faithful people are actively serving God through the traditional institution. Such service is praiseworthy and necessary. My critical attention is not intended to negate any work that God's Spirit inspires. Instead, my desire is to question the present structure of the church and compare it with a different organizational vision—one that Jesus may have had for his bride.

The content of this book spans over 3,000 years of church history. I travel back in time, to gather some important organizational clues from some of the earliest writings in the Bible. Looking back in time helps us to move forward with clarity. The larger picture provides an understanding of where the church *has been*, where she is *today*, what she must change, and where she *could go*—if changes were made.

I begin the discussion by painting a backdrop of information, against which organizational issues are then presented. Once the backdrop is in place, my focus turns to locating the image of an organizational structure within the words of sacred text. After *The Net* has been located in its scriptural context, I examine a collection of Jesus' teachings that relate to the topic of organization.

As the discussion progresses, early organizational efforts in the book of Acts are mentioned, followed by a brief look at a few of the relevant images in the book of Revelation. I then move on to the spiritual components of *The Net*; how it might function as an organizational structure for grassroots ministry; and how the church might envision using *The Net* in the future.

Throughout the book, I discuss numeric groupings that are intrinsically attached to *The Net* and its teachings. I've chosen to use numerals, in lieu of spelling out numeric values, when the numerals refer to the organizational groupings within *The Net*. This stylistic choice allows for visual clarity and ease of recognition on the page.

Lastly, this book includes many fishing concepts. I suspect that Jesus chose a few good fishermen, as his disciples, because they possessed a net-making skill that Jesus wanted to employ. The church cannot spread a net, or cast a net, until she organizes herself in the image of a net. Furthermore, if the church is to successfully fill her net, she must first learn how to *become* a net.

Yes, the spiritual air is swirling!

Yes, change can be both frightening and exhilarating!

These are exciting times, indeed!

How shall we respond?

Prologue

The Winds of Change

As a theologian, I find it helpful to have a sense of context out of which an author's opinions and perceptions arise—especially when interpreting the Bible. I also find it helpful to understand an author's personal perceptions or biases when reading their work. Perceptions obviously influence the content of every book. Thus, in an effort to be transparent, I will disclose my biases followed by a big-picture perspective regarding the spiritual shift that I believe we, God's people, are experiencing.

Theological Leanings

I write from a theologically moderate position. I choose to position myself in the middle of the theological garden because, for me, it is a spiritually healthy place to reside. I respect the history of sacred text. I am fascinated by the different textual sources that were collected, merged together, and preserved. I enjoy the wide spectrum of literary forms that make up the scriptural tapestry—from the mythological, poetic, allegorical, metaphorical, symbolic, visionary, and prophetic—to the historically verifiable.

Overall, I desire to keep an open mind when I read, study, and research sacred text. Having said that, the material in this book is visionary in nature, symbolic in imagery, yet literal in application. My research on the subject of organization taught me a critical lesson: it's easy to conclude that certain aspects of Scripture are purely symbolic when a literal application has not been disclosed, isn't overtly obvious, or is not within one's ability to comprehend. I've learned that it is possible for both literal and symbolic meanings to happily coexist within the same passage, story, or vision in the Bible.

Regardless of my theological opinions, discernment is always necessary when reading the works of theologians or scholars who interpret sacred text. A solid foundation of reason and evidence must accompany our thinking as we share insights with one another.

Personal Perceptions

Three concepts seem important to mention in preparation for the information in this book: (1) a transfiguration of the church is underway and irreversible, (2) we are entering a season when spiritual roots will deepen, and (3) the Bible may have more to teach us through a different lens.

I've chosen to use the word *transfiguration* because it infers a change beyond what human effort could cause, manipulate, or imagine. The use of this term invokes the image of the transfigured Christ, which is my intention. At the time of the transfiguration, the disciples, who witnessed the phenomenon, described a change in Jesus' clothing! "His clothes became dazzling white, whiter than anyone in the world could bleach them" (Mark 9:3 New Revised Standard Version).

In the same way, I believe that the church will be transfigured during this time of intense spiritual change. I believe she will appear newly clothed in a heavenly way as time unfolds. The clothing worn by the church is her image in the world—her *dress*. Thus, a transfiguration of the church would involve a change in the outward appearance of the church universal. Since the church is made up of God's people, we should probably expect to see an adjustment in human activity—not a change of fleshly appearance—but a modification of direction, mission, language, organization, and discernment of time.

People who have been called out of the traditional church are ordinary souls who are trying to be obedient to the movement of God's Spirit within their own hearts and minds. They are preparing for a new day in the life of the church by reimagining a different future for the church. Such thinking is important because it encourages open mindedness.

Reimagining exercises help people discern the direction of the spiritual winds. They serve to determine the centeredness of God's Spirit within the shift. Knowing that the changes within the church are *God-led* and *God-inspired* may provide a measure of comfort for those who don't understand why things can't be the way they used to be. Likewise, it is helpful to realize that the traditional church must remain intact until a new ministerial model exists in a functional, knowable way.

In truth, most people will not abandon an organization—even one that has become somewhat dysfunctional—if something viable is not presented as an option. Instinct prevents people from jumping off of a wind-battered ship without seeing dry land within swimming distance. Therefore, those who have been called out of the church of yesterday must plan for the church of tomorrow in tangible, visible ways *before* expecting large numbers of people to migrate.

The Shipwreck

It may be helpful to consider the shipwreck off the coast of Malta, Acts 27:27, as an analogy for the present condition of the institutional church. In this account, we are introduced to gale-force winds that had blown the ship far off course. To save the vessel, the sailors unloaded their cargo. When that didn't help, they let go of the ship's tackle. When that wasn't enough to control the ship, their focus changed from saving the vessel, to saving the lives of the ship's passengers. After turning to prayer, they tossed their grain into the sea in preparation for their life-saving swim to an unknown land at daybreak. So, a concerted effort was made to save the ship, but when that was not possible, all attention shifted to saving human lives.

The process of letting go is scary for many people. Nothing feels right about it unless letting go is perceived as the only way to save lives. Many people do not yet perceive the inevitability of the church's institutional demise. It must be made clear, however, that the people of God don't fall apart in the analogy of the shipwreck. It is the *ship* that falls apart while everyone on board survives! In other words, it would be the church's present organizational structure that eventually collapses, while people of faith survive the collapse and migrate to a different organizational model. That's the type of radical, life-saving change that we should expect to experience as the church is transfigured!

Most Christians who have been called out of the traditional institution *do* see the vulnerability of an institutional collapse. In fact, many faithful people look forward to the breakdown of the institutional model with hope, because it would be viewed as a mark of spiritual growth and progress. Countless souls have already begun to let go of practices that have become burdensome, doctrines that no longer seem relevant, and old assumptions that are now realized as spiritually unhealthy ideas (excessive attention to sinfulness, disproportionate feelings of guilt, undue attention to the salvation of others resulting in a violation of spiritual boundaries, establishment of doctrines of right believing, etc.)

The *doctrine of right believing* is particularly troubling because it produces the side-effect of self-righteousness. The notion that everyone must agree on the *right* beliefs about God, Jesus, or God's Spirit, has caused incredible division among Christians. The idea that there *is* one right way to believe, has splintered the Christian faith tradition into far too many factions. This notion is part of the church's burdensome cargo that must be released into the sea of yesterday.

As the Spirit moves within hearts and minds, people have begun to rid the ship of all unnecessary baggage that has been accumulated on the journey to date. Not everyone, however, has been called to let go of traditional teachings or practices. This is a good thing! As previously stated, the present institutional structure must remain somewhat intact, while those who are called to organize the church of tomorrow search for ways to build a knowable entity.

Seeing an Unknown Land

During the search, soundings must be taken, just as the sailors in Acts 27:27–28 took soundings in the dark of night. At midnight, the sailors sensed that they were approaching land. The soundings confirmed their perceptions as the depth of water became increasingly shallow. At that point, the sailors dropped anchor and waited for daybreak.

When the light of dawn allowed them to physically see the land, the ship's passengers and crew jumped into the water. Those who could swim made it to the shore without assistance. Those who could not swim were instructed to take broken boards from the ship and float toward the land. We must take note, however, that no one recognized the land to which they swam or floated.

Christians should expect the same. The process of transfiguration will carry God's people to an unknown place of thinking, being, and doing. We should anticipate radical change, not only in *organizational* matters, but also a change in *language* and the church's *perception of time*. We would do well to help people trust in the healing power of God in the midst of this intense spiritual change.

While we are preparing each other, one important question will naturally surface time and again: "If everything from the past ends up in the sea of yesterday—to what unknown entity do people swim?" Searching for the answer to that question will lead us forward, one step at a time. Whatever the church's transformed image is to be, it must be perceived, not only as a means of spiritual survival, but also, as a welcomed relief from certain calamity! God's people must understand that a transfiguration will provide a pathway toward an exciting new beginning!

Deepening Spiritual Roots

In the above analogy of the shipwreck, we realize that the passengers spent the entire winter season on the island of Malta before setting sail again. As reported in Acts 28:9, much healing took place among the islanders who were sick. Although the Bible doesn't mention it, we can imagine that a different type of healing occurred among those who swam to shore from the sinking vessel. When lives are saved, hierarchies tend to disappear. We can be certain that the pilot, crew, soldiers, passengers, and prisoners, adopted a more egalitarian attitude toward each other during their island respite. Thus, it is safe to say that both physical and spiritual healings were part of the winter experience for everyone on the island.

I expect that the transfiguration of the church will also include a season, during which hierarchies will tumble, spiritual roots will deepen, and healing will take place.

The season will resemble a conceptual winter—a period of time when the root systems of trees are actively energized *below* the surface of the ground. The present season of the church, which is now ending, has been marked by the full-colored splendor of showy, autumn foliage such as: stately buildings, colorful robes, embroidered stoles, lavish pipe organs, stained-glass windows, and well-ordered processionals or recessionals with much pomp and circumstance, etc.

All of that will change as the season changes. The church's winter will be marked by a barren outward appearance. Above the surface of the ground, the church may *appear* dead, but she will be fully alive. She will be energized in non-visible ways. Her roots will deepen *in anticipation* of future buds, flowers, and fruit. True to the parable of the sower, the church of tomorrow will finally be able to sow her seeds "into good soil" (Mark 4:8). Having sown in three previous soils that did not produce the desired results, the church will finally be able to produce her intended yield. In the meantime, she must discern a change of seasons, from autumn to winter.

As the church endures her winter, she must do so with a hefty dose of humility. A humble soul thinks of himself as no better or worse than any other soul. Humility has always been a *virtue*, but considering the spiritual shift that is underway, humility will become a *necessity*. When people believe that they know everything there is to know, a change in perception is often resisted in favor of retaining control over the known. On the other hand, a true spirit of humility enables people to think and feel with the mind and heart of a child—full of wonder and eager to learn, adapt, and trust.

The First Net Makers

A humble attitude does not require that we leave our brains behind, however. No! Intellect is required for spiritual discernment and deep rooted thinking. Having said among biblical scholars regarding whether we have come to an end of discovery about the Bible. A credible study of sacred text employs a criteria known as the historical-critical lens. It has served the scholarly community well. We know things about sacred texts that we would never know were it not for the research conducted through this lens.

However, another criteria exists by which credible study could be accomplished—the lens of light, color, and image. We know that oral cultures relied heavily on light, color, and image, when perceiving their world. So, why not consider this primal form of communication when examining the words of sacred text—words that paint pictures for us!

The lens of light, color, and image, illuminates a parallel realm of insight that runs congruent with the historical-critical lens. It is a complementary lens that rides like a passenger in the sidecar of the historical-critical motorcycle. (If a mental picture of a sidecar on a motorcycle was created, when reading the previous sentence; then, the lens of light, color, and image was just employed.)

Human beings first learned to communicate by creating picture stories based on observances of light, color, and images of nature. Written languages were then created to communicate and preserve thoughts. Today, in order to gain additional insight regarding the words of sacred text, we must reverse the process by converting the language of words back into the language of pictures. Much information can be gleaned when considering ancient words and their corresponding images.

Painting mental pictures, to complement some of the verses found in sacred text, is essential if we have any hope of discovering the organizational image of *The Net* contained in this book. *The Net* becomes visible only when we draw a picture that corresponds with the descriptive words. Having mentioned this, we should not wonder whether we have come to an end of discovery concerning sacred text. We may be nearing the end of insight through the historical-critical motorcycle, but a vast realm of discovery rides in its sidecar. We simply need to acknowledge that God isn't finished with us yet. The Bible has more to reveal through a different lens—if we are willing to look.

Concluding Sentiments

It is my hope that this backdrop of information, along with a transparency of personal perceptions, was helpful in preparing people for a discussion about organizational change. I believe the image of *The Net*, contained in this book, is something that must be considered as the wind of God's Spirit carries us into the church of tomorrow. Spiritual matters require discernment, which can only occur over a slow pondering of ideas and insights. Progression is almost always a meditation by meditation journey. Having said that, I invite people to read the subsequent material slowly, think deeply about the information provided, and keep an open mind.

PART I

Discovering *The* Net

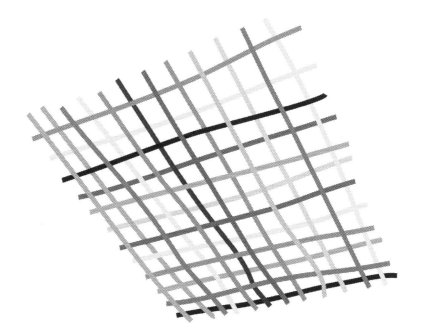

1

Feeding the Multitude

Discovering *The Net* begins with an examination of the two miracle feedings as recorded in the New Testament. The feeding of the 5,000 is recorded in all four gospels, while the feeding of 4,000 is only found in Mark and Matthew. This fact is unfortunate because it leads many people to think that the feeding of the 5,000 is, somehow, *more important* than the feeding of the 4,000—an assumption that we may want to toss overboard. As I will demonstrate, the two miracle feedings are of equal importance, and best viewed as one complete teaching.

The feeding of the 5,000 will send us back in time, to see an organizational aspect of Jewish tradition through Jesus' eyes. The feeding of the 4,000 will lead us forward, from the time of Jesus, to see the vision he established for the church triumphant. Thus, the discovery process begins in the *middle* of the scriptural tapestry. And so we begin . . .

Mark 6:30–44

Jesus and the disciples went by boat to a remote place. They wanted to separate from the crowds that had gathered around them earlier in the day. Due to the coming and going of the crowds, they hadn't had a chance to eat. So, Jesus suggested that they retreat to a quiet place. Unbeknown to them, a crowd of people ran on foot from various towns and villages, only to arrive at the remote place ahead of them. Hence, they were unable to eat, and quiet time was not possible.

Mark's account mentions that Jesus felt compassion for this crowd because "they were like sheep without a shepherd" (Mark 6:34b). So, he began to teach them many things, but we have no knowledge of the things Jesus taught preceding the feeding of the 5,000. When the hour was late, the disciples came to Jesus saying, "Send them away so that they may go to the surrounding country and villages and buy something for themselves to eat" (Mark 6:36).

It's important to note that the shepherd-less people did not come to Jesus complaining of physical hunger. We can discern, therefore, that this account reveals two *different* forms of hunger. Jesus and the disciples were physically hungry, but the crowd hungered after spiritual food! The two forms of hunger create a dichotomy within the text: the disciples wanted to *send people away* to get food, while the crowd wanted to *gather together*, with Jesus and his disciples, to satisfy their hunger.

You Feed Them!

Aware of their spiritual need, Jesus refused to send the shepherd-less crowd away. Using the opportunity to teach the disciples how to satisfy a non-physical form of hunger, Jesus turned to his disciples and said, "You give them something to eat" (Mark 6:37). The disciples replied, "Are we to go and buy two hundred denarii worth of bread, and give it to them to eat?" (Mark 6:37b).

Again, the disciples reveal their concern over literal bread and money. The disciples didn't believe they could do what Jesus had asked them to do! Furthermore, spending that much money to feed a crowd of people (who just happened to show up) didn't seem to appeal to the disciples. After all, the spontaneous gathering prevented the disciples from eating earlier in the day!

Apparently, Jesus had a bigger picture in mind when he said, "You give them something to eat." We know it as an ancient proverb: Give people a fish and they will have food for a day; teach people to fish and they will have food for a lifetime. Through hindsight, we can deduce that Jesus wanted to teach the disciples how to provide food for a lifetime. His interest wasn't limited to satisfying physical hunger without also addressing spiritual needs.

Counting Loaves

Jesus asked, "How many loaves have you? Go and see." When the disciples found out, they said, "Five—and two fish" (Mark 6:38). Thus, the miracle begins with the nourishment that the disciples had. (For the purpose of this discussion our focus will remain on bread.)

At this point in the story, symbolism begins to play an important role. Mark mentions that the disciples told the people to sit down on the green grass. While the color, green, may seem like an insignificant detail, the green grass indicates the presence of living, growing, fertile, vegetation. It's one of those visual clues in the Bible that is full of spiritual implications. The shepherd-less people sat down on a living, growing surface—a *spiritually fertile* environment! The detail, gleaned through the lens of light, color, and image, foreshadows the multiplication of bread that was about to take place.

Furthermore, Mark provides us with another exceptionally important detail. He reveals that the people sat in groups of 100s and 50s. We don't know if Jesus initiated the grouping, or if the people chose to group themselves. Nevertheless, this numeric arrangement points directly to the ancient words in Scripture that illuminate *The Net*—the original organization of God's people. The groupings of 100s and 50s reflect the tribal organization in the Sinai Desert during the Exodus.

At this junction, therefore, we must leave the groups of 100s and 50s on the green grass, while we go back in time to the sacred stories of Jesus' boyhood tradition. We will return to the miracle feeding after examining some key organizational factors within Judaic history.

Let the flashback begin!

Jethro said . . .

The account of Jethro's visit to Moses pinpoints the scriptural location of the original organization of God's people. In context, the people of Israel had been released from slavery in Egypt, yet they had difficulties governing themselves, once liberated. After all, Pharaoh's government dictated every aspect of their lives for 400 years! But suddenly they had no government at all—except for the still, small voice of God through the voice of Moses.

Like children, the Israelites needed guidance. When disputes arose, they turned to Moses for resolution. Long lines of people waited to speak to Moses from morning 'til night. When Moses' father-in-law, Jethro, saw the lines of people, he asked why Moses acted alone as judge. Moses said, "Because the people come to me to inquire of God" (Exodus 18:15). Jethro replied . . .

> "What you are doing is not good. You will surely wear yourself out, both you and these people with you. For the task is too heavy for you; you cannot do it alone. Now listen to me. I will give you counsel, and

God be with you. You should represent the people before God and you should bring their cases before God; teach them the statutes and instructions and make known to them the way they are to go and the things they are to do. You should also look for able men among all the people, men who fear God, are trustworthy, and hate dishonest gain; set such men over them as officers over thousands, hundreds, fifties, and tens" (Exodus 18:17–21).

From these words, we are able to discern that Jethro laid out an organizational plan, which ultimately gathered the tribal communities together for the good of caring for each other. His plan also included holding each other accountable for respectful behavior under God's Law! Jethro wanted Moses to teach God's Law, but he also wanted Moses to empower the Israelites to govern themselves autonomously with those laws. Such thinking would have been incredibly unique in comparison with the lack of autonomy under Pharaoh's government. Nevertheless, Moses saw the wisdom in Jethro's organizational plan and agreed to implement the idea.

Some scholars suggest that the Exodus out of Egypt may be a mythological story of faith rather than an historical event because, at this point in time, no archeological evidence has been discovered to support such a mass exodus. Regardless of its literal historicity, Jethro's organizational structure serves as an interesting leadership model. As Christians, however, we have not been taught to appreciate its value. Likewise, we've missed the connection between this organizational model, and the miracle feedings of the 5,000 and 4,000.

Organization's Groupings

In due course, the organizational structure laid out by Jethro, brought God's Law together with God's people in one tightly-woven network of human community. The resulting organization divided people into groups of 1,000s, 100s, 50s, and 10s. The largest number in Jethro's division was 1,000s. The Bible does not clarify whether the 1,000s are individuals or families. That's okay. The largest group of 1,000s is most likely an approximate division of the overall population.

That being said, we could consider Jethro's numeric divisions in the following way:

- The largest group of 1,000s is the equivalent of a small community of people within a larger tribe, town, city, etc. One trustworthy leader is chosen to represent the needs or concerns of the community of 1,000s—the equivalent of a rabbi or pastor.
- From within the 1,000s, another trustworthy leader represents a smaller group of 100s. This person would be the equivalent of an associate pastor or rabbi. The smaller group of 100s becomes the organizational image of *The Net* of 100—similar to the size of many congregations that tend to the spiritual needs of their community of 1,000s, today.
- *The Net* of 100, is then divided in half with two additional trustworthy leaders representing two smaller groups of 50. These two groups represent God's Law, written on two legendary tablets, as will be shown. Thus, the two groups of 50s have no similar equivalent in our churches, today.
- *The Net* of 100 is also divided into twenty smaller groups of 10s. Trustworthy leaders are chosen to represent these groups. Today, the smallest groups would

be the equivalent of traditional church committees, or teams, that serve in the various aspects of ministry such as fellowship, education, and evangelism, etc. However, *The Net* of 100 functions in a different way, which will be imparted throughout this book.

The division of leadership is a basic breakdown of numbers—one community of 1,000, one team of 100 people, two teams of 50 people, and twenty teams of 10 people—or 1,000s, 100s, 50s, and 10s. The community of 1,000s has its representative, while each of the smaller teams have their representatives—*twenty-four trustworthy representatives* from within *The Net* of 100 people.

This division of labor defines the organization of God's people in a way not too dissimilar from the organization of the church today. But the organization is woven together in a distinctively different way, as shown in the illustration that follows. The other major difference, is the way in which the structure is cast out over spiritual waters, which will be the main focus of Part II of this book.

The Net of 100

The image below is a square of 100 people, represented by 100 circles. The illustration offers a bare-bones look at *The Net* of 100 and its 10 by 10 square of human leadership. At this early point in the discussion, I want to call attention to the *horizontal* and *vertical* lines that make up the design. *The Net* resembles a piece of cloth, woven together with horizontal and vertical threads. Each thread in the organizational structure represents the small groups of 10s. The entire *cloth* represents the larger group of 100s—a well-ordered pattern for connected leadership.

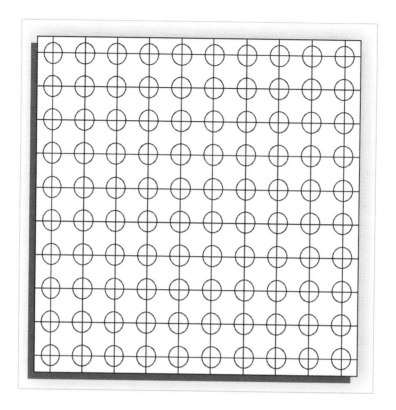

Net of 100s

The Horizontal Lines and the Ten Commandments

Each horizontal line represents one of the Ten Commandments, as shown in the next illustration. *The Net* of 100 people is divided into two smaller groups of 50 people each. One group of 50 represents five commandments, as shown *below* the dotted line. The second group of 50 represents the other five commandments, as shown *above* the dotted line. Again, these two groups symbolize the two tablets and the Ten Commandments.

This illustration also features the first covering over the tabernacle, which was woven from three different colors of "blue, purple and scarlet" thread (Exodus 26:1–6).

The resulting covering, shown in grayscale, was actually a fine, *purple* linen. I've chosen to feature the first covering, in this drawing, because its overall design corresponds perfectly with the organizational divisions within *The Net* of 100; namely, the groups of 50s and 10s.

The first covering was constructed of ten woven panels—divided into two sections of five panels each. The two sets of panels were held together by 50 blue loops sewn on one set of panels, and 50 blue loops sewn on the other set—100 blue loops in all. Fifty gold clasps joined the blue loops together, making one continuous covering. All in all, the covering mirrors the precise image of the organizational structure of God's people in groups of 100s, 50s, and 10s. This covering also symbolizes the Ten Commandments, divided into two tablets of five commandments each, as shown below.

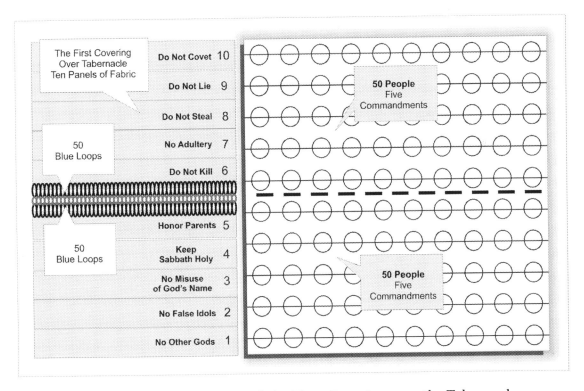

The Ten Commandments and the First Covering over the Tabernacle

Three Different Sources

It is important to note that Jethro's organizational structure, the Ten Commandments, and the first covering over the tabernacle, were provided by three different literary sources at slightly different times in Israel's history.[1] The account of Jethro is derived from the E source—an early school of thought that emerged from the northern kingdom, which elevated God's name, Elohim. The Ten Commandments came from an unknown source—a separate document inserted into the scriptural text. The pattern for the tabernacle and its coverings originated from the P source, which emerged at a later point in time from within the Jerusalem priesthood.

In spite of the separate sources and different time periods, it becomes clear from the illustration above, that all three sources were upholding and validating the same information concerning this 10 by 10 organizational structure. If three different sources upheld the same information, we can deduce that the original organization of God's people was no small matter within ancient Israel.

However, it is nearly impossible to discern the relationship between Jethro's organization, the Commandments, and the first covering, without bringing all three aspects together in one illustration. This is an example of the insight to be gleaned when examining sacred text through the lens of light, color and image. We must convert the words of ancient text into pictures in order to *see* their descriptive elements!

The Vertical Lines and the Human Lifecycle

Next, we move on to the vertical lines in the organization. An issue of great importance to the ancient Israelites was the preservation and sanctity of human life within tribal

---

[1] Friedman, Richard Elliott. *The Bible with Sources Revealed.* New York, NY: Harper Collins, 2003

society. The ten vertical lines in the illustration below, indicate ten, age-related groupings within the lifecycle. *The Net* of 100, with their twenty-four trustworthy representatives, would look after the various needs of the people—from the newly born infants to the elderly. The lifecycle most likely indicates spiritual growth, from infancy to maturity, as well. It was important for God's Law to be upheld by every tribal member throughout the entirety of life—a birth to death commitment!

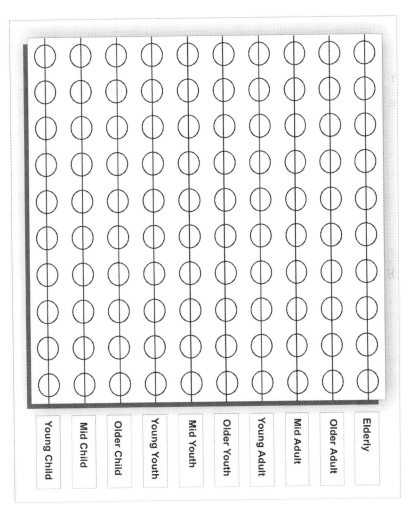

The Human Lifecycle

The Complete Net of 100

When completed, *The Net* of 100 creates a spiritual intersection between God's Law and God's people. When joined together, within *The Net* of 100, the combination reflects a closely-knit, interconnected organization, as shown below. It is a 10 by 10 structure that teaches God's law to God's people at every age.

By studying the illustration below, it can be determined that each person serving within *The Net* focuses on a specific task consisting of one commandment and one age group! It is a dual focus created by the intersections of horizontal and vertical lines. Thus, the Law and the lifecycle merge together for one unified purpose.

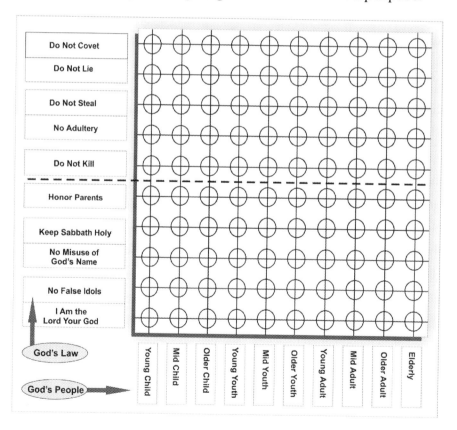

The Complete Net of 100

The Vision of a Net

This completed illustration of *The Net* is the image that floated between my face and the windshield of our car, as described in the preface of this book. I saw horizontal and vertical lines, which I initially perceived as an administrative tool for organizing different aspects of ministry. I didn't realize that it was an actual organization of people! Therefore, the image that I saw did not contain 100 circles. The image only contained horizontal and vertical lines. Later, when I learned that the image was Jethro's organizational model for the tribes of Israel, I added the 100 circles to represent human leadership.

When the image first appeared before me, the Ten Commandments were not part of the grid, either. Instead, I saw different categories of ministry such as: Worship, Creative Arts, Fellowship, Recreation, Education, Nurture, Discernment, Stewardship, Evangelism, and Mission. At the moment of its revealing, I was taken aback by the completeness of its design, as each category of ministry intersected with every age in the human lifecycle. I have since realized that traditional church ministries relate to the Ten Commandments, but time has dimmed the relationship, causing a somewhat convoluted connection between ministry and Law.

The Pattern of the Tabernacle

I also realized that Jethro's organizational structure, with its horizontal and vertical lines, relates closely to the frames, projections, and crossbars in the pattern of the tabernacle. The reason for noticing the imagery of the ancient tabernacle is to establish consistency of ancient thought and design. Using horizontal lines and vertical lines is a common factor in both the organizational structure of God's people as well as the pattern for the tabernacle.

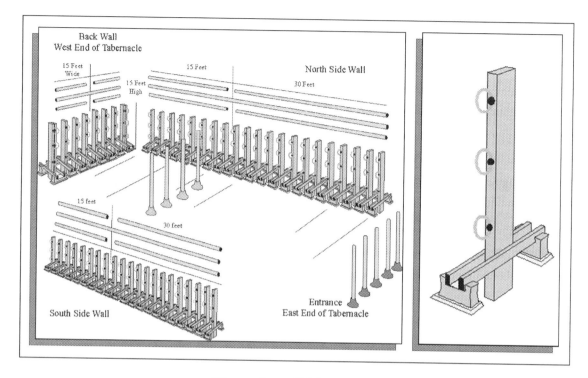

Dissection of Tabernacle

All things considered, we should marvel at the spiritual connectedness that is promoted through the interweaving of horizontal and vertical lines. The imagery clearly points to a picture of strength and solidarity. As Christians, we would be remiss if we did not appreciate the symbolism of the horizontal and vertical lines! The image of the cross of Christ is also a symbol of strength and solidarity. It represents our connectedness within the body of Christ. Sadly though, Christians have not understood that these intersecting lines also represent an organized structure that brings God's Law and God's people together.

End of flashback!

Basic Arithmetic

Meanwhile, back on the green grass, the spiritually hungry crowd just sat down in groups of 100s and 50s. Now we know exactly why this particular grouping was important! It reflected the organizational model of Jesus' spiritual tradition—a legacy that had been passed from generation to generation through the sacred stories in the Torah. Jesus did nothing to dismantle, reject, or abandon the seating arrangement.

As the account continues, Jesus lifted up the five loaves of bread, blessed them, and broke the loaves. Then, he handed the *ten* broken loaves to the disciples to set before the people. While painting a mental picture of Jesus breaking five loaves of bread, we may want to ask and answer the following questions:

- o How many pieces of bread were set before the people? [10]
- o How many commandments are represented by the groups of 100s and 50s? [10]
- o How many age-related groups are represented in the organization? [10]
- o How many people serve in the smallest groups in *The Net* of 100? [10]
- o How many panels of cloth were used to make the first covering over the tabernacle? [10]

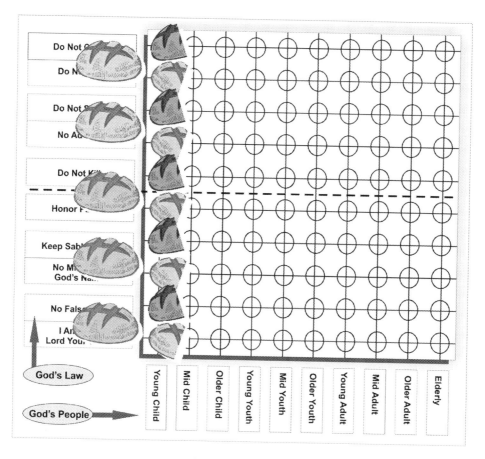

The Five Loaves

The key to understanding the connection between the ancient organization of God's people and the miracle feeding of the 5,000, is to notice—not five loaves—but *ten broken loaves*! Ten, is the number that must be perceived in order to discern that the loaves of bread, Jethro's organizational structure, the Ten Commandments, and the first covering over the tabernacle are, in fact, related to each other! All images are based on 10s.

During the distribution of bread, each person would have taken their portion of the broken loaves, thereby ensuring that everyone in each group of 100s and 50s would be fed. And now we know exactly what Jesus was feeding to the shepherd-less crowd of people—the Ten Commandments! Thus, Jesus fulfilled their spiritual hunger by teaching the shepherd-less crowd the Commandments while passing blessed and broken nourishment from one person to another.

Jesus showed us how a spiritual feeding is done! It's accomplished through a bread-passing method that Jesus frequently repeated. Luke recounts a time when Jesus broke bread during the last supper saying, "Do this in remembrance of me" (Luke 22:19b). The teaching-feeding concept continues to this day, but Christians do not relate the method to the Ten Commandments or to an organizational structure that could feed 1,000s!

In this same manner, we must envision the shepherd-less crowd of 100s and 50s, passing bread within their larger communities of 1,000s—thereby feeding 5,000 people! When the crowd returned to their respective towns and villages, we can imagine them saying, "We ran after Jesus, and we learned about God's Law as we passed broken loaves of bread among us. We sat on the green grass in groups of 100s and 50s. Then, we listened, and talked, and laughed, and . . ."

It helps to perceive this miracle through the eyes of those who were asked to seat themselves in groups of 100s and 50s. The fact that Jesus engaged the seating arrangement is also insightful. The feeding provides a glimpse into Jesus' organizational vision for the church and his desire to empower people—not only to feed themselves, but to pass the feeding on to others.

Who knows how many people literally took a small pinch of bread as the broken loaves passed from one person to another! Does it matter? No! Five loaves were broken. Ten pieces of bread were distributed, and 5,000 people were fed. That's miraculous. That's the spiritual power of a closely-knit organization of people who have learned how to nourish their communities of 1,000s!

Claiming the Church that Jesus Claimed

As I've listened to a variety of reimagining exercises over the past fifteen years, I've sensed a desire, on the part of many Christians, to rethink the organic nature of the first church in the book of Acts. To date, however, I haven't detected a desire to revisit the Mosaic encampment and claim the church that Jesus claimed.

Although Christianity began 2,000 years ago, after the resurrection of Jesus, the church as an organization of God's people was born much earlier in the Sinai Desert. Christians often dismiss the foundational aspects of the Jewish faith, as recorded in the Pentateuch—the first five books of the Hebrew Bible—because we believe that Jesus made all things new. Why return to old, or former, thinking!

Additionally, Christians often assume that a new covenant, through Jesus, made God's Law obsolete. But sacred text does not support these assumptions. As will be shown in the next miracle feeding, the old covenant of Law was *sealed* with a new covenant, while the Law itself remained fully viable. Consider the following words of Scripture:

> "Do not think that I have come to abolish the law or the prophets; I have come not to abolish but to fulfill. For truly I tell you, until heaven and earth pass away, not one letter, not one stroke of a letter, will pass from the law until all is accomplished. Therefore, whoever breaks one of the least of these commandments, and teaches others to do the same, will be called least in the kingdom of heaven; but whoever does them and teaches them will be called great in the kingdom of heaven" (Matthew 5:17–19).

Unfortunately, Christianity's reluctance to place too much emphasis on the Ten Commandments hinders people from embracing the goodness of God's Law, along with the ancient organizational structure that upheld it.

Was the church a rebellious, bratty child under the old covenant of Law? Yes. Was she raised by parents who went too far by adding law after law to the original Ten Commandments? Yes. Did she feel trapped under hierarchical thinking and behaviors that would not let her become the loving organization she was meant to become? Yes! For these reasons and more, Jesus needed to rescue the church, heal her, and set her free from wrongful human control.

Over the course of more than a thousand years—prior to the life and times of Jesus—Judaism morphed into a legalistic institution of traditions, rituals, and practices of right believing and behaving. In spite of this fact, Jesus never rejected Judaism. He rejected what Judaism had become under Pharisaical leadership, but he honored the church's organizational birth in the desert of Sinai. He respected her original structure of 1,000s, 100s, 50s, and 10s, and he spent much of his earthly ministry redirecting God's people toward a spirit of love, as will be discussed in the next chapter.

Before moving on, however, it must be stated that Christianity has also morphed into a legalistic institution of traditions, rituals, and practices of right believing and behaving. Christianity is a mirrored image of the misguided condition of Judaism—the environment into which Jesus entered human history. Having said that, Christians must see themselves in an identical light with the Jewish people of Jesus' day.

Today, many Christians are walking away from the church's institutional image, practices, teachings, and traditions for the same reason that Jesus criticized the religious practices of his day. Like Jesus, such 'defectors' are not rejecting Christianity. *They reject what Christianity has become.* Many people know that the church must, once again, be released from wrongful human control. She must be healed. Her course must be redirected if she is to fulfill the vision Jesus had for the bride of Christ.

One aspect of healing, that must take place within the church of today, involves looking back in time—all the way back to the original birth of the church on earth! Christians must embrace the organizational model that Jesus embraced when feeding the spiritually hungry crowd that was seated on the green grass in groups of 100s and 50s. To understand God's original plan, Christians must revisit the Exodus in Sinai, and claim the church that Jesus claimed!

The Leftovers

To conclude the feeding of the 5,000, we must consider another mathematical issue. When the crowd had been satisfied, Mark tells us that twelve baskets full of leftover pieces were collected by the disciples. No matter how we calculate the twelve baskets, nothing adds up. If five loaves were passed among the crowd; then, five baskets full of pieces might make sense. If ten *broken* loaves were passed; then, ten baskets full of pieces might make sense. Yet, twelve baskets do not correspond with the five loaves, the ten broken loaves, or the organizational model of 1,000s, 100s 50s, and 10s. Something is wrong with this picture!

Scholars might suggest that the twelve baskets symbolically represent the twelve disciples—the sending out of the twelve—as recorded in Mark 6:7. While a strong symbolic tie to the twelve disciples is likely, it does not point to the possibility that Jesus wasn't finished teaching!

I assert that the number of leftover baskets is intentionally linked to the second miracle feeding of the 4,000. The twelve baskets suggest an incomplete scenario at the end of the feeding of the 5,000. But the enigma could be solved if the two miracle feedings are joined together as one complete teaching. This possibility will be discussed in the next chapter.

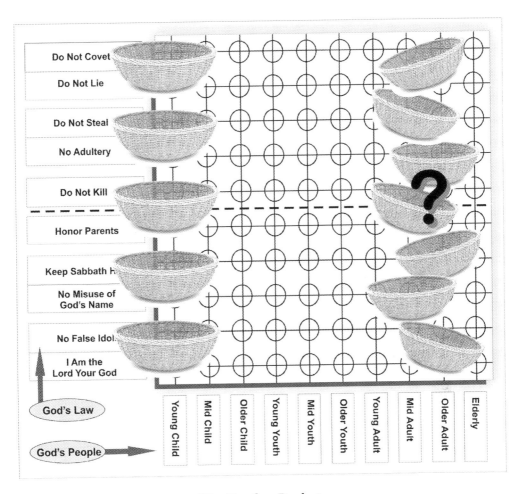

The Twelve Baskets

2

Feeding the Multitude—Again

As mentioned previously, the feeding of the 5,000 is often thought to be more important than the feeding of the 4,000. If Jesus was able to feed 5,000 people with five loaves of bread, why couldn't he feed 4,000 people with seven loaves? Think about it! A smaller crowd . . . more bread! On the surface, the feeding of 4,000 just doesn't seem as impressive as the feeding of 5,000.

But perhaps Jesus wasn't trying to impress anyone. Perhaps he was in the process of teaching something powerful—something that required *two lessons* rather than one! Perhaps the two feedings indicate an important aspect of growth, change, and spiritual fulfillment of Jesus' purpose on earth. To comprehend the full value of his teachings, I suggest that the two feedings must be deemed *inseparable*. I've discovered, however, that the feeding of the 4,000 requires a greater depth of discernment regarding organizational issues.

Let's revisit the second miracle.

Mark 8:1–10

Jesus and the disciples were teaching a large crowd of people, some of whom had traveled a long distance to be with them. This group of people is different from the shepherd-less flock of 5,000. That particular group stayed with Jesus and the disciples for a few hours, while this large crowd stayed with Jesus for three days!

The length of time is symbolically important. Had they planned for their long trip and their lengthy stay? If they planned ahead, how much food did the sojourners bring with them? Enough for three days—plus the food that would be needed for their homeward journey?

Like the teaching that preceded the feeding of the 5,000, we know nothing about the things Jesus taught prior to the feeding of the 4,000. All we know is that Jesus felt compassion for the people—not because they were like sheep without a shepherd—but because they stayed with him for so long. These people had obviously found their shepherd in Jesus. They were his fans and followers! No one travels a long distance to be with someone they don't like; then, stay with that person for three days.

Sensing their need, Jesus called to his disciples and said, "I have compassion for the crowd, because they have been with me now for three days and have nothing to eat. If I send them away hungry to their homes, they will faint on the way—and some of them have come from a great distance" (Mark 8:3).

With this information, we can assume that the crowd had digested much food for thought during their stay. Nevertheless, before sending them away, Jesus wanted to give them something substantial for their homeward journey—something that would sustain them on the road.

Counting Loaves—Again

Like the feeding of the 5,000, the gathering of 4,000 occurred in a remote place. Again, the disciples ask, "How can one feed these people with bread here in the desert?" (Mark 8:4). Again, Jesus asked the disciples, "How many loaves do you have?" "Seven," they replied, (Mark 8:5). (A few fish are mentioned further on in the reading, but for the purpose of this discussion, our focus will remain on the seven loaves of bread.)

When considering the feeding of the 5,000 and 4,000 together, we realize that the two feedings were accomplished with 12 loaves of bread—five loaves distributed in the first feeding, plus seven loaves distributed in the second feeding, or 5 + 7 = 12. Remember that a total of 12 baskets of leftover pieces were collected after the feeding of the 5,000. Thus, the two miracles are joined together by the 12 leftover baskets. Now, the 12 baskets full of leftover pieces make perfect sense!

With this simple equation in front of us, we can deduce that five of the baskets represented the five loaves that were fed to the 5,000. The remaining seven baskets *projected the future number of loaves* needed for the feeding of the 4,000! We can also deduce that the number, 12, represents a *future* organizational number just as, 10, represents a *past* organizational number.

At this point, we may want to ask the following mathematic questions:

- If five loaves of bread fed 5,000 people, why are seven loaves needed to feed 4,000?
- How would Jesus use the two extra loaves?
- When seven loaves are broken, to what end would the fourteen *broken* loaves be used?
- Would ten broken loaves be used as they were in the previous feeding?
- If so, how would Jesus use the four remaining pieces?

While this feeding appears to present a mathematical puzzle, it is actually an *organizational* riddle that must be solved! This calls for discernment. Wouldn't Jesus logically employ the same organizational structure in both miracle feedings?

Presumably so! However, when Jesus asked the crowd to sit down, there is no indication from Mark's account of the 4,000, that the people seated themselves in groups of 100s and 50s.

Matthew's account of the 4,000 reflects Mark's words almost verbatim. So, the two gospel writers have not offered any clue as to how the bread was distributed in the second miracle feeding. Nevertheless, if the feeding of the 5,000 *preceded* the feeding of the 4,000, we can deduce that the same organizational structure was employed in both feedings, as shown below.

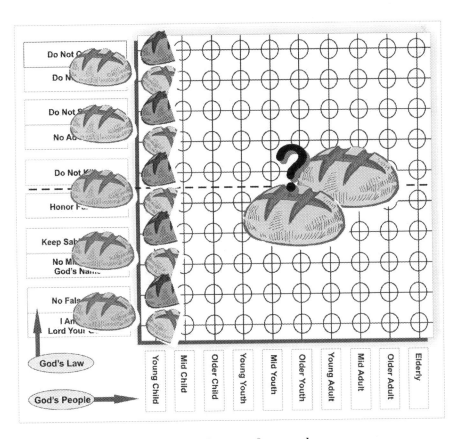

The Seven Loaves Incomplete

Would an increase in the number of loaves suggest an increase in the size of the organizational structure of *The Net*? Yes. But why? *The Net* features the Ten Commandments and the entire human lifecycle from infancy to elderly. Thus, the original *Net* of 100 is complete, in and of itself. Nothing more is needed. Why would Jesus want to add anything to the Ten Commandments? This is the organizational riddle that must be solved.

Just as we needed to look back in time, during the feeding of the 5,000, in order to pick up an organizational clue from Jesus' boyhood tradition—now we must look ahead in time. Since Jesus was sending some of the 4,000 people on a long-distance journey, we must also look into the future through a long-distance lens. We can do this by considering the entire scriptural context in which the feeding of the 4,000 took place. In doing so, we will examine Jesus' relationship with the Pharisees, and the Law, itself.

Let the projection begin . . .

A Sign from Heaven, Mark 8:11–12

Skipping ahead in time, we discover that Jesus and the disciples went by boat to a different region *immediately following* the feeding of the 4,000. After arriving in the region, the Pharisees came to Jesus to test him. They asked for a sign from heaven. Jesus sighed deeply in his spirit and said, "Why does this generation ask for a miraculous sign? Truly I tell you, no sign will be given to this generation" (Mark 8:12).

We can only guess that the news about Jesus' teaching spread rapidly since the prior feeding of the 5,000. There he was—at it, again—feeding another multitude! The fact that the Pharisees came to test Jesus suggests that he had done something to upset them. What might that *something* have been?

We don't know all of the things that Jesus taught. But we do know, as his ministry grew in popularity, some of the religious authorities perceived him as a threat to the religious and social order. If Jesus employed Jethro's organizational model to feed 5,000 people, it would have become clear to the religious authorities that he was empowering people with the Ten Commandments—in a completely new way. No one in authority would have wanted a popular itinerant preacher to organize large groups of people based on a different perspective of God's Law! Those who had been given authority to teach and enforce the laws would have wanted their tradition to be kept intact.

Looking at Jesus from the Pharisees' perspective, organizational efforts would have seemed disturbing—particularly when those efforts took place in remote places. Why was Jesus teaching in a clandestine manner? This calls for discernment! Why did large crowds gather in remote places to learn from Jesus? Why did they travel long distances to meet Jesus in those remote places?

Why is Mark the only writer that mentions groups of 100s and 50s? This one detail is the lone scriptural thread that ties Jethro's organizational structure to the feeding of the 5,000. Without this tiny clue, no connection is possible. Even with the clue, one must discern that the tribal organization was a weaving together of God's Law with God's people. The woven organizational structure must then be applied to the miracle feeding!

This amount of insight requires deep thinking and understanding. Like many important aspects of Jesus' teachings, this one can only be discerned with the help of God's Spirit, because the combination of insights are obscured by the enormity of words in the scriptural tapestry.

In truth, however, we shouldn't wonder why the organization of large groups is not overtly mentioned in the gospels. Jesus was forced to teach in remote places, because he taught personal empowerment to insiders, within Judaism, as well as outsiders. Jesus knew that his teachings would ruffle feathers and upset social apple carts. Therefore, he had no choice but to teach as quietly as possible.

I would conclude that he kept his teachings hidden from view in order to buy time. Only the passage of time would allow him to reach as many people as possible with his egalitarian ideology. Thus, we hear Jesus say, "Tell no one about what they had seen until . . ." (Mark 9:9), or strict orders that "no one should know this" (Mark 5:43).

When considering the fuller picture, we become aware of the fact that Jesus taught people to view God's Law through the spirit of inclusion—the spirit intended by the Law! But the scribes and Pharisees had adopted a legalistic viewpoint of exclusion—the spirit *not* intended. Yet, a legalistic approach to God's Law worked! It kept sinners and outsiders in low social positions, while the Pharisees enjoyed the perks of a higher social status.

To be fair, these religious leaders acted as they thought they should. They were the ones in charge of conserving and preserving holiness! A legalistic approach was believed to be necessary in order to retain a sense of righteousness and purity before God. Much of Christianity is practiced with this same mindset, today. But Jesus didn't approve of this approach in the Jewish tradition, nor should Christians, as followers of his teachings.

Jesus perceived legalism to be a distortion of a rightful spirit of love within Judaism. Legalism turned God's Law upside down and inside out. Therefore, Jesus' mission in ministry was to invert the negative turnover and make things right-side-up again! Returning God's Law to its rightful spiritual intention would allow the Ten Commandments to work *for* people, instead of *against* them. Needless to say, Jesus' mission was nothing short of heroic!

The mission was also incredibly dangerous. As an insider, Jesus used his wisdom, knowledge, and insight to challenge the authorities within his own faith tradition. Yet, the same teachings could ultimately dismantle the well-established power structures within the whole of society. Jesus' mission did not position him on a pathway toward popularity. It placed him on the fast track to crucifixion.

It's no wonder that some of Jesus' teachings were wildly contested in comparison with others. We can't blame Jesus for teaching organizational matters in secret. We can't criticize the gospel writers for choosing their words carefully—writing about teachings that were benign—while offering crumbs, tidbits, or vague hints about teachings that were less benign.

Likewise, it's only natural that the Pharisees showed up in hot pursuit of Jesus by the time that the second feeding of 4,000 was completed. We can only imagine their anger! "Prove to us that you have the authority to teach the things you are teaching! Come on! We want a sign from heaven! Why do you think you are a better teacher than those of us who have studied the Torah for years? Who gave you the right to imply that our teachings are wrong or harmful?"

Nevertheless, Jesus refused to give them a sign. He was determined to complete his mission of correcting the misuse of God's Law. The Ten Commandments were believed to be a supreme gift from God that should be embraced with joy—not rules that must be followed in fear. The Commandments were to be celebrated as God's path toward successful living—not cursed as a burden that is too heavy to carry. They were meant to benefit everyone—not just Jewish insiders. God's Law was meant to empower all who wished to embrace it!

The Most Important Commandment

We do not know the chronology of Jesus' teachings. The four gospels provide no particular order. What teachings came *before* others? Which parables were taught first? Which ones were taught toward the end of Jesus' ministry? We simply don't know the succession of Jesus' lesson plan. Therefore, it is impossible to discern *when* Jesus was questioned about the most important commandment. We only know that, at some point in time, one of the teachers of the Law asked, "Which commandment is the first of all?" (Mark 12:28b).

> Jesus answered, "The first is, 'Hear, O Israel: the Lord our God, the Lord is one; you shall love the Lord your God with all your heart, and with all your soul, and with all your mind, and with all your strength.' The second is this: 'You shall love your neighbor as yourself.' There is no other commandment greater than these" (Mark 12:28–31).

Jesus quoted directly from the Torah. Answering the question in this way, Jesus called attention to the spiritual bond between the teacher, who asked the question, and himself. He persuaded this teacher to see the *One God* they had in common, instead of focusing on the fact that they did not agree on Jesus' liberating approach to the Law. The teacher had no choice but to acknowledge the truth of Jesus' answer and agree with him. In doing so, the teacher humbled himself. All hierarchical arrogance melted from his heart.

End of projection!

Framing the Old to Become the New

This brings us back to the feeding of the 4,000. Now that we've looked at the big picture perspective of Jesus' relationship with God's Law—as well as the relationship that the Pharisees had with the Law—we can return to the large crowd preparing to leave for their long-distance journey. We left the scriptural scene with some questions in mind: "What additional sustenance would Jesus want to give his followers? Why would Jesus want to add anything to the Ten Commandments and the organizational structure?"

Based on Jesus' relationship with The Ten Commandments; his response to the Pharisees regarding a sign; and his response to the teacher who was testing him—it's fair to deduce that Jesus wanted to add *two loaves of love* as sustenance for the homeward journey. We can discern, therefore, that the two additional loaves of bread symbolized the two laws of love that Jesus quoted from the Torah. "Love the Lord your God with all your heart and with all your soul and with all your mind and with all your strength" (Deuteronomy 6:4). "Love your neighbor as yourself" (Leviticus 19:18).

As shown below, the two loaves of bread, which were broken into four pieces, *sealed* the organization with a four-sided frame of love, when distributed equally within the structure. In order to frame the Ten Commandments with the two laws of love, Jesus needed two extra loaves of bread—seven loaves in all. When Jesus lifted up the seven loaves, blessed them, and broke them, the disciples would have had *fourteen pieces of bread* to set before the people.

Thus, fourteen pieces of bread would have been distributed. Ten broken pieces represented the Ten Commandments. Four broken pieces framed the organizational square. In doing so, Jesus increased the size of the organization from *The Net* of 100 to *The Net* of 144. In doing so, the organizational divisions were changed from 1,000s, 100s, 50s, and 10s, to 1,000s, 144s, 72s, and 12s. (The largest group of 1,000s remained the same, as this group represents a generic tribal grouping rather than a specific leadership grouping in *The Net*.)

Thus, the overall organization is changed from a 10 by 10 square, to a 12 by 12 square—another reason for twelve baskets, and twelve loaves of bread—and the choosing of twelve disciples. By increasing the size of the structure, Jesus surrounded the organization with love. But it is important to note that he did not change *The Net* of 100 trustworthy representatives. The original net remained intact! Jesus simply added a frame around the original design, thereby *sealing* God's Law with love!

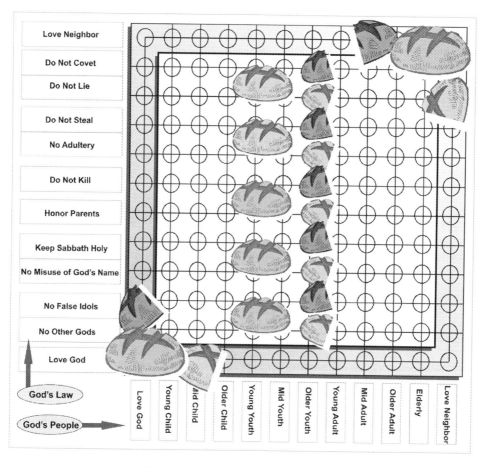

The Seven Loaves Completed

Arithmetic—Again

By adding the two laws of love to the Ten Commandments, during the feeding of the 4,000, Jesus completed a new organizational vision for God's people! Sustenance for the long, journey home was provided, and all were satisfied. The miracle isn't complete, however, until the disciples pick up the leftovers. "They [the disciples] took up the broken pieces left over, seven baskets in all" (Mark 8:8b).

Think about the picture that Mark paints for us. The disciples had seven loaves of bread at the beginning of the feeding. When all were satisfied, seven baskets full of broken pieces were leftover. No one left the scene wanting anything more. In fact, the seven baskets indicate enough food for another feeding!

Yes. That's exactly the point. We can deduce that there will forever be seven leftover baskets full of bits and pieces after all are satisfied. The seven loaves, and seven leftover baskets, establish the concept of a *perpetual* feeding—from crowd to crowd, and generation to generation. Seven loaves. Seven baskets. Seven loaves. Seven baskets. With this conclusion, the two miracle feedings are complete.

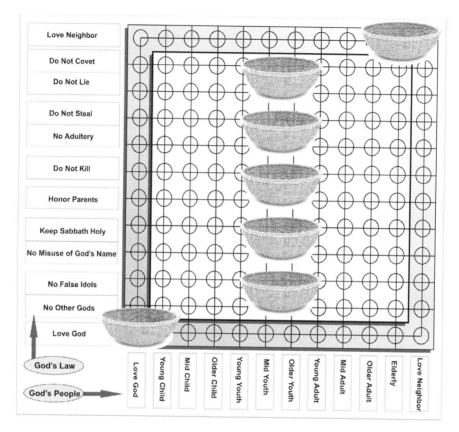

The Seven Baskets

The Church's Homeward Journey

Just as the feeding of the 5,000 required a return to the Mosaic encampment in the book of Exodus, the feeding of the 4,000 requires a forward projection in time. We projected forward in time, from the feeding of the 4,000 to the Pharisees' request for a sign from heaven. Now we will look even further ahead to the image of the church triumphant in the book of Revelation.

The two feedings, when combined into one complete teaching, reveal both the past image of the church, in her infancy, and the future image of the church, in her state of spiritual maturity. When Jesus framed *The Net* with love, the old covenant of Law was *sealed* with a new covenant of love that embraced God's Law in its entirety. It's important to reiterate that the new covenant of love did not abolish God's Law. It simply made the first covenant obsolete by *sealing* it with a new covenant.

Metaphorically speaking, it could be said that the crowd of 4,000 represents the church on her long-distance journey—a journey that the church is still experiencing! In other words, the crowd of 4,000 symbolizes us—the fans and followers of Jesus who come from near and far, stay with him for three days, learn from him, but are then sent on a homeward journey. When we read the account of Jesus sending the crowd away, it is as if he is sending the church on her journey to become who she is intended to become—an organization built on Law and love!

But we have the benefit of looking through the lens of hindsight. The crowd of 4,000 didn't have the lens that we now have. Neither did the disciples. Projecting forward, from the miracle feeding, we can see the image of the New Jerusalem "coming down out of heaven from God, prepared as a bride adorned for her husband" (Revelation 21:2). We know that this is the church's future image. We know that this is the long-distance destination to which the bride is traveling! Nevertheless, Jesus' disciples couldn't have known that John of Patmos would see such a vision, many years after Jesus' death, and then eventually write about a bride adorned for her husband.

John also writes, "The city lies foursquare" (Revelation 21:16). The city is described as measuring 12,000 stadia in length, height and width, with walls that were 144 cubits, by man's measurement. Hence, the New Jerusalem is a 12,000 x 12,000 x 12,000 cube, measured in stadia, and 144 cubits thick. The literal measurements are symbolic, but they point to a cube-shaped organizational structure, based on 12s and squared on all sides! John's vision describes the organizational image of the church—from the time of Jesus, onward. His description is a 12 by 12, square-shaped image.

In review, it is important to realize that the organization of God's people began with groups of 1,000s, 100s, 50s and 10s; then, increased to groups of 144s, 72s, and 12s. We can safely conclude, therefore, that the increased size of the organization was Jesus' future vision for the church. It was to become her *bridal dress* under the new covenant of love— her new way of ministering to communities of 1,000s from the time of Jesus, forward.

Each person that takes part in her organization of Law and love, is like a pearl on her wedding gown. The image of an organizational square of trustworthy leaders, having no desire for personal gain, is shown below. This is the wedding dress that the bride of Christ must agree to wear, if she is to fulfill the words of Scripture. Is the church currently dressed in this way? If not, is she willing to organize herself in this way? If not, why not?

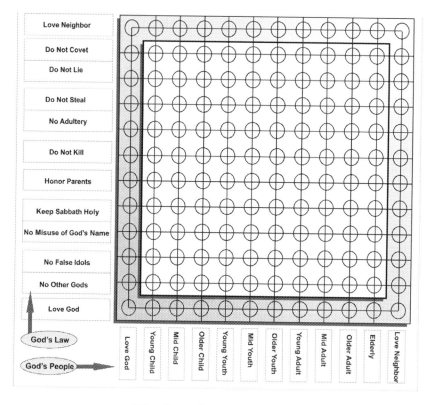

The Complete Net of 144

3

The Problem with Yeast

Now that *The Net* has been discovered in the words of sacred text, we must discuss why the organizational vision, given to us by Jesus, and visualized by John of Patmos, is not part of Christian awareness. What happened to the vision? Why did it disappear? This chapter will offer some insight into the disappearance of *The Net* of 144, as we discuss human behavior.

We pick up the story where we left Jesus in a different region—*after* the feeding of the 4,000, and *after* the Pharisees asked him for a sign from heaven. Jesus told them there would be no sign. After their demands were refused, Jesus and the disciples returned to their boat. This time they traveled to the other side of the Sea of Galilee.

Crossing the sea must have given Jesus time to think about what had just happened during his encounter with the Pharisees. Reflecting on the questioning that took place, Jesus may have sensed a turning point in his ministry. We can't know what Jesus may have been thinking, but while they were in the boat, he shared the following concern with his disciples.

Mark 8:14–21

"Watch out—beware of the yeast of the Pharisees and the yeast of Herod" (Mark 8:15). As king of Judea, Herod possessed secular authority, just as the Pharisees enjoyed religious authority. It's possible that Jesus was merely concerned about the Pharisees' request for a sign. It's also likely that he perceived a deeper, more troubling issue, bubbling up beneath their request. Whatever Jesus was thinking at the moment, it gave him cause to say, "Beware of the yeast."

Oblivious to the true nature of Jesus' warning, the disciples chatted among themselves. "It is because we have no bread" (Mark 8:16). Mark mentions that the disciples forgot to bring bread with them, so they only had one loaf in the boat. When Jesus heard the disciples' fretfulness over their lack of bread, he immediately questioned them by asking, "Why are you talking about having no bread?" (Mark 8:17).

When reading this account, we can't help but have compassion for Jesus! Balancing on a spiritual high-wire must have been mentally exhausting for him. On the one hand, he was forced to cope with self-righteous leaders who perceived his teachings as a growing threat. On the other hand, he had chosen twelve naïve men who viewed their teacher with a growing sense of awe, while they remained somewhat clueless.

We can only imagine that Jesus' rise in popularity became both a blessing and a burden by the time the two miracle feedings were completed. From the perspective of the Pharisees and Herod, an itinerant preacher, teaching faith stories about the kingdom of heaven, would have seemed harmless. However, empowering people to organize in groups, *under the government of God's Law*, instead of Herod's law, or Pharisaical authority, would have intimidated both secular and religious leaders.

Jesus's teachings elevated people's self-esteem to the point of feeling spiritually equal to their authorities—a preposterous idea! He helped people realize that God's Law could be a gift, rather than a club used against them. Jesus knew that such activity would appear suspicious to the Pharisees, as well as Herod.

Patiently, however, Jesus continued to question his disciples. "Do you still not perceive or understand? Are your hearts hardened? Do you have eyes, and fail to see? Do you have ears, and fail to hear?" (Mark 8:17–18a). The ongoing rebuking was necessary because Jesus wanted to open the disciples' eyes and ears concerning the problem of yeast. Everything he had imparted during the two miracle feedings could be completely undermined by the growth of yeast. Jesus understood this.

Persistently, he drilled his disciples, "And do you not remember? When I broke the five loaves for the five thousand, how many baskets full of broken pieces did you collect?" They said to him, "Twelve" (Mark 8:18b–19). Their concern over a lack of bread proved to Jesus that the spiritual significance of his teaching, during the feeding of the 5,000, had alluded them. He obviously wanted the twelve leftover baskets to imprint on the disciples' minds. These were Jesus' home-grown net makers! Did they not comprehend their role in building the future church?

"And the seven for the four thousand, how many baskets full of broken pieces did you collect?" And they said to him, "Seven" (Mark 8:20). Again, Jesus referred to the number of baskets. Why would his disciples be concerned about a lack of bread? The seven baskets full of leftover pieces indicated a perpetual supply of bread. The organizational vision for the future church on earth had been imparted. Didn't the disciples understand their net-making task? Couldn't they put themselves into the picture Jesus painted before their eyes?

We can only imagine Jesus' exasperating thoughts! "Guys! Wake up! I'm not concerned about literal bread! You will never run out of bread if you organize yourselves the way I showed you! God's Law will guide you and a spirit of love will sustain you. Don't you get it?"

But Jesus simply asked, "Do you not yet understand?" (Mark 8:21).

No! They didn't! And sadly, Christians haven't understood the spiritual significance of the two miracle feedings, either. The organizational efforts of Jesus have alluded us. Like the disciples, we have not put ourselves into the picture Jesus painted during the two miracle feedings of 5,000 and 4,000 souls. Like the disciples, we have eyes and ears that have failed us.

However, we can be certain that the Pharisees *had* placed themselves into the picture Jesus painted. Their eyes were wide open! As religious leaders, they enjoyed a distorted sense of authority. The scribes and Pharisees perceived themselves as the righteous leaders of God's chosen people. They believed it was their duty to enforce God's Law and preserve the exclusiveness of their spiritual and social status as Jews. Consequently, they saw their positions of authority rapidly vanishing if Jesus continued teaching, organizing, and empowering people with his inclusive perspective of God's Law!

Like many of today's religious leaders, the authorities in Jesus' day would have been blind to the injustices of their own actions. They would not have perceived themselves as promoters of exclusivism. Instead, they would have perceived themselves as protectors of purity. Wouldn't God want the chosen people of Israel to remain *separate* from sinners and outsiders in order to remain spiritually pure? Yes? No?

The answer to this question challenges us to see the fine line of distinction that lies between promoting exclusivism and protecting purity! In the tiniest crevices of human thinking—yeast can grow and become a major problem.

Human Air

The harmful growth of yeast could destroy all organizational efforts from the outside. Likewise, the presence of yeast can destroy an organization from within. Yeast fills everyone's spiritual bread with so much human air that there is no room for God's Spirit to work, move, teach, or inspire, etc. Human air takes over in places and spaces where God's Spirit would otherwise live and breathe.

Filling empty areas, where God's Spirit could move and thrive, is the definitive problem with yeast! Its swelling habit causes mental and spiritual elevation in the human mind, resulting in attitudes of pompousness, arrogance, and egotism. It causes people to think more highly of themselves than is appropriate. It leads to a misuse and abuse of power. It tricks people, who have been given authority, into saying and doing unthinkable wrongs, in order to preserve a sense of righteousness or spiritual purity. In worst case scenarios, yeast is the root cause of war, murder, genocide . . . .

The Yeast of Today

Intellectually speaking, many people understand Jesus' inclusive teachings. Yet such honorable ideals quickly disappear when people become members of a religious organization such as a temple, church, or mosque. When birds of a feather flock together, it becomes easy for people to believe that one's particular group has a better, more enlightened view of spiritual matters when comparing their views with others.

From the Christian perspective, it is tempting to enjoy the sense of personal empowerment that comes from accepting Jesus, as Savior of the world. Personal empowerment is precisely what Jesus offered through a right relationship with God's Law and a new covenant of love. Nevertheless, if even a tiny amount of harmful yeast enters into personal empowerment, one's thinking can easily turn into a wrong-headed *self-righteousness*. When Christians seek to gather together in exclusive groups of agreement, these groups can quickly begin to think that their beliefs are superior to all other beliefs about God, Jesus, or the Spirit of God.

Such arrogance encourages Christians to think of themselves as spiritually *saved* while perceiving others as *unsaved*. When Christianity is viewed from the perspective of the outsider, it seems preposterous to think that any human being could judge the spiritual condition of another person's soul. When Christians attempt to do so, such arrogance overshadows good intentions—mirroring the yeast in the minds of the Pharisees with whom Jesus had to cope. The scribes and Pharisees considered themselves to be spiritually *chosen* while judging others as sinners or unclean people who were not favored by God.

Jesus viewed this growth of yeast as harmful—something that deserved a warning. The growth of this type of yeast seems especially problematic within the practice of monotheism. The spirit of humility is supposed to be at the heart of monotheism, but self-righteousness often prevails where a spirit of humility would otherwise thrive. The goodness of monotheism is easily distorted by the growth of yeast within one's mind, heart, and spirit. It can quickly contaminate an otherwise healthy spiritual life. When that happens, the contamination is often passed from generation to generation—expanding in size as it passes. This is the essence of the warning Jesus gave about the yeast of the Pharisees. "Watch out," Jesus said.

Personal Empowerment for Collective Good

One major difference existed between Jesus' heart, and the hearts of the Pharisees and Herod. The difference can be summed up as a lack of fear in Jesus' heart, and the presence of fear in the hearts of the authorities. Through the lens of hindsight, we know that Jesus wasn't organizing people to rise up against their religious and secular governments. He wasn't equipping armies of people with weapons! He wasn't preaching hatred. He wasn't promoting rebellion. He wasn't instigating riots in the streets! He wasn't plotting an overthrow.

Jesus wasn't feeding people with yeast-filled ideas. In fact, many times Jesus asked people to return to their homes in silence after they had been with him. Nevertheless, the leaders and rulers of Jesus' day were obviously afraid of his growing popularity. Even though a physical overthrow of the social order was never intended, the authorities evidently believed that Jesus' teachings could provide a pathway toward a militaristic uprising. Therefore, it shouldn't surprise us that the authorities of Jesus' day began to fear his teachings and view his growing popularity as a potential threat.

In truth, Jesus merely tried to empower individuals for personal good. He provided them with an organizational structure from his own faith tradition, and he taught a bread-passing method that could improve the lives of everyone in their communities. The organization of people was a grassroots effort designed to bring neighbors together for the good of their neighborhood—period.

It was designed to help *average* people see a pathway toward a better life, in spite of their social status in the religious or secular landscape of their time. His teachings elevated those of low degree to the point of *equality*—not *superiority*! He taught personal empowerment for the collective good of society—not for the purpose of overthrowing their religious leaders or their secular governments.

Jesus knew that the pathway toward spiritual wholeness and wellbeing starts within the tribal community in which each individual is born. If *The Net* of 144 could supply spiritual nourishment to local tribe of 1,000s, then the whole of society would become healthier. Nevertheless, Jesus said, "Watch out." Yeast is the one ingredient that could spoil the bread-filled miracle. *And it did*!

4

Three Parables

As previously mentioned, some of the seemingly benign teachings of Jesus relate to the organizational structure of *The Net*. But we, as Christians, have not perceived such connections. This chapter highlights three of Jesus' parables that relate to the original *Net* of 100—the lost sheep, the lost coin, and the lost son. These parables provide additional evidence that Jesus openly referred to Jethro's organizational structure during his ministry.

The gospel of Luke features these three parables together. Furthermore, Luke reveals the audience that Jesus addressed when speaking. "Now all the tax collectors and sinners were coming near to him [Jesus]. And the Pharisees and the scribes were grumbling and saying, 'This fellow welcomes sinners and eats with them'" (Luke 15:1–2).

The grumbling of the Pharisees reveals a few things about their spiritual attitudes. It's obvious that they didn't see themselves as sinners. Welcoming sinners was thought to be shameful. Eating with sinners was appalling. The scribes and Pharisees expected Jesus to uphold acceptable social and religious behavior, but his popularity among *outsiders* provoked them.

The Parable of the Lost Sheep, Luke 15:1–7

With this backdrop in place, Jesus told the parable of the lost sheep. In essence, the parable is an organizational lesson that posed a spiritual challenge for the Pharisees and teachers of the Law to consider.

> "Which one of you, having a hundred sheep and losing one of them, does not leave the ninety-nine in the wilderness and go after the one that is lost until he finds it? When he has found it, he lays it on his shoulders and rejoices. And when he comes home, he calls together his friends and neighbors, saying to them, 'Rejoice with me; for I have found my sheep that was lost.' Just so, I tell you, there will be more joy in heaven over one sinner who repents than over ninety-nine righteous persons who need no repentance" (Luke 15:4–7).

By intentionally selecting the numeric group of 100 sheep, Jesus transported his audience back to the tribal organization of 1,000s, 100s, 50s and 10s. The group of 100 taught the Law and held the tribes together as a tightly-woven society. Thus, the 100 sheep symbolize *The Net* of 100 that joins God's Law to God's people.

Notice that Jesus didn't begin with the assumption that the lost sheep was an *outsider* who begged to be included in the group of 100. No! The lost sheep was an *insider* within *The Net* of 100! "Which one of *you*, having a hundred sheep and losing one of them . . ." In other words, Jesus painted the sinner *into* the tightly-knit organizational structure, thereby implying that the sinner could be someone who served as a trustworthy leader among them. The sinner could be a Pharisee or a scribe!

This parable isn't an innocent story about a cute, little lamb who was lost. The deeper issues of inclusion, exclusion, self-righteousness, and spiritual blindness, lie at the heart of this parable. Jesus presents a challenge that addresses the subject of who is, and who is not, welcome in the organization of God's people! Likewise, it challenges those within the organization to wonder who among them might be lost!

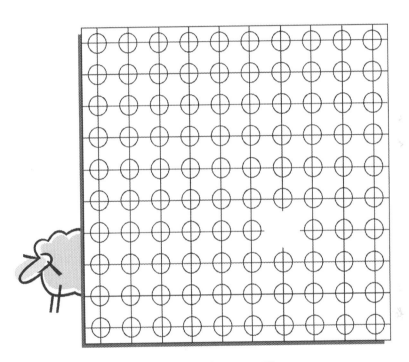

The Parable of the Lost Sheep

Jesus knew that the scribes and Pharisees saw no need to repent of their self-righteous ways. He knew all about the yeast that permeated their thinking. So he posed a question that would position the leaders and teachers between a rock and a hard place. If they answered, "Sure we'd leave the ninety-nine in the open countryside to look for the one who was lost! Everyone is needed in the group of 100s!" In doing so, they would implicate themselves as the grumbling hypocrites that they had become.

If they answered, "No! We'd rather stay with the ninety-nine who aren't lost!" In that case, their attitude of self-righteousness would be revealed. Additionally, they would expose their willingness to compromise the integrity of their tightly-woven organization. In other words, the lost sheep would create a hole in *The Net* of 100, but they would be content to live with that outcome.

To be certain, Jesus pinned the Pharisees into an uncomfortable spot because he painted the sinner *into* the organizational structure! They could either view themselves as hypocrites, or see themselves as unconcerned leaders who would allow their close-knit organization to unravel—one lost sheep at a time.

Knowing that the question could not be answered without self-incrimination, Jesus proceeded to lather on the sweetness of finding a lost sheep and joyfully placing it on one's shoulders. For the benefit of those who were on the outside looking in, Jesus drew a loving, mental picture of the whole tribe, gathering together to wildly rejoice over the return of one missing sheep. How awesome that portrayal would have seemed to those in Jesus' audience who had experienced nothing but rejection from religious leaders! Who, among the listeners on that day, could have resisted the warm, inviting picture Jesus painted?

The Parable of the Lost Coin, Luke 15:8–10

We should be slightly amused at Jesus' tenacity. He couldn't let the organizational lesson end with the parable of the lost sheep. No! He persisted with his spiritual challenge by creating another scenario for the Pharisees and teachers of God's Law to consider. This time, Jesus focused his attention on the smallest group of 10s in *The Net* of 100.

"Or what woman having ten silver coins, if she loses one of them, does not light a lamp, sweep the house, and search carefully until she finds it? When she has found it, she calls together her friends and neighbors, saying, 'Rejoice with me, for I have found the coin that I had lost.' Just so, I tell you, there is joy in the presence of the angels of God over one sinner who repents" (Luke 15:8–10).

This story calls attention to one's immediate group of 10s, in the organizational structure of 100s, 50s, and 10s. These are the people with whom eye contact is made on a regular basis during organizational meetings. But it also calls attention to the woman who owns the coins.

A shift in ownership occurs between the first and second parable. The parable of the lost sheep began with the question, "Suppose one of *you* . . ." Thus, the owner of the sheep could be anyone in Jesus' audience. The parable of the lost coin began with the question, "What *woman* . . ." This can't be just anyone in Jesus' audience. It must be *a woman* who loses something of value.

Suppose one of these 10 coins is lost! Would it matter to the other nine people, in the group of 10s, if one of their *church leaders* couldn't be found? To what length would the Pharisees go to find the person with whom eye contact has been made? Would they light a lamp in order to search? Would they clean their spiritual house? Or would they simply say, "That's okay. We have nine other people. Besides, we don't need, *or like*, that person anyway."

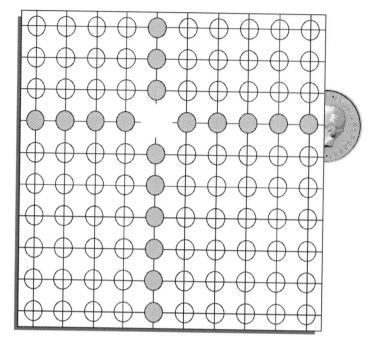

The Parable of the Lost Coin

Again, Jesus posed a question that would position the scribes and Pharisees between a rock and a hard place. If they answered, "Sure we'd light our lamps and sweep our house in order to find a valuable coin! Every coin is needed in the group of 10." Again, they would implicate themselves as grumbling hypocrites.

On the other hand, if they answered, "No! We'd rather stay with the nine valuable coins that aren't lost. We'd prefer to operate our dusty organization in the dark." In that case, they would reveal their self-righteous attitudes. And once again, they would expose their willingness to lessen the value of a closely-knit organization. In other words, the lost coin would create another hole in *The Net* of 100, but they would be content with that outcome.

Because Jesus positioned the lost coin in the smallest organizational group of 10s, the Pharisees and teachers of God's Law could either view themselves as dusty housekeepers, who wouldn't waste time lighting lamps, or they could see themselves as leaders who would willingly compromise the strength and integrity of their organization—one lost coin at a time.

For the second time, Jesus proceeded to lather on the sweetness of the desired outcome of this parable. He treated his audience to a delightful portrayal of a woman [the church] who gathers all of her friends together, that they might enthusiastically rejoice over the lost coin she has found. While the entire community celebrates with her, Jesus says, "I tell you there is joy in the presence of the angels of God over one sinner who repents!"

We can only imagine that Jesus may have looked straight into the eyes of the scribes and Pharisees when he spoke those words.

The Lost Son, Luke 15:11–32

After telling the previous parables, Jesus continued with the infamous story of the prodigal son. This parable would have been particularly stinging to the ears of the scribes and Pharisees, but the story does not mention any specific numeric groupings in the organization of God's people. Instead, Jesus elevates the organization to that of a grand estate! He also reveals that the owner of the estate is a *father*.

Notice the shift in ownership again. The 100 sheep belonged to anyone. The 10 coins were owned by a woman—the *church*. And the grand estate is owned by a *father*—presumably God. The shift in ownership moves the audience from a sense of personal accountability for sheep, to the church's accountability for her valuable coins. In the final parable, the father is accountable for all who inherit a portion of the grand estate—the kingdom of God. Each shift of ownership promotes a deeper sense of connectedness to *something*, or *someone*, with a wider scope of influence.

The parable of the lost son begins with the spiritual disorientation of a child who inherited wealth from his father, but chose to leave his father's estate in order to go his own way in the world.

> Jesus said, "There was a man who had two sons. The younger of them said to his father, 'Father, give me the share of the property that will belong to me.' So he divided his property between them. A few days later the younger son gathered all he had and traveled to a distant country, and there he squandered his property in dissolute living" (Luke 15:11–13).

Since we know Jesus' audience, we could deduce that he was indirectly accusing the scribes and Pharisees of abandoning the work of God and squandering their spiritual inheritance as a chosen people of God. Did Jesus hope that these spiritual leaders would insert themselves into the story of the lost son? Did he want them to realize the extent of rejoicing that would take place if they returned to the rightful work of their heavenly father? Did he want them to become more invested in the impartiality of God's estate, and the vastness of God's mercy?

Concluding Thoughts

By combining the illustrations of *The Net* of 100 with the picture stories of the lost sheep and the lost coin, we can conclude that both parables correspond with the numeric groupings in Jethro's original organizational structure of 1,000s, 100s, 50s, and 10s. On the other hand, the parable of the lost son points to the work that must be done within the whole kingdom of God.

The three parables are noteworthy. Each story brings about a potential dilemma regarding organizational matters; namely, people who walk away from the organization, or become lost for undisclosed reasons. Thankfully, Luke saw the importance of pulling these three stories together as one continuous teaching. We can deduce, therefore, that he was aware of the organizational connection between these stories.

The parables also validate the importance of every human being who participates in an organization. The parable of the lost sheep reveals the significance of everyone who serves in the group of 100s. The parable of the lost coin demonstrates the value of each person in the groups of 10s. The parable of the lost son demonstrates the value of each person who works in the vastness of God's earthly kingdom!

We can be certain that *personal value* was Jesus' main thrust when he told these particular parables. If the Pharisees and teachers of the Law would focus their attention on personal value, they just might stop grumbling about Jesus' relationship with sinners and tax collectors!

Lastly, the attention Jesus gave to the groups of 100s and 10s in these parables, suggests that he treasured the organization of the church. After all, the church is Jesus' bride. His attention to her structure reveals his desire to uphold the spiritual integrity of her organizational image. Yet we, as Christians, do not teach the organizational aspects of these parables, because our eyes have not been opened to the organizational perspective.

5

Acts and Visions

When addressing an audience that included scribes and Pharisees, Jesus referred to *The Net* of 100's, 50s, and 10s. At other times, Matthew, Mark, and Luke mention groups of 12s. Luke also mentions a group of 72. Both numbers, 12 and 72, point to *The Net* of 144 that Jesus implemented during the feeding of the 4,000.

It can be deduced, therefore, that Jesus referred to the *Net* of 100 when addressing audiences that identified with its 10 by 10 structure—the church's *original* image. When privately mentoring his disciples, however, he would have focused on the 12 by 12 structure—the church's *future* image. This chapter focuses on additional biblical evidence that supports *The Net* of 144.

The Twelve and the Seventy-Two

Three years of mentoring and teaching helped the disciples understand the depth and scope of their unique spiritual call. During those three years, the gospel writers state that Jesus sent the disciples out as a group—*the sending out of the twelve*. Luke mentions that Jesus also appointed a group of seventy-two whom he sent out in pairs. The following accounts record both appointments: Mark 6:7, Matthew 10, Luke 9:1–5 and Luke 10:1–23.

The twelve disciples reflect the number of people in the smallest groups within *The Net* of 144. The increase, from groups of 10 to groups of 12, guaranteed that each group of 10 would have two additional people feeding their group with the laws of love—the love of God and the love of neighbor. Hence, *The Net* of 144 consists of 12 groups with 12 people in each group.

In addition to the twelve apostles, Luke writes, "After this, the Lord appointed seventy others and sent them on ahead of him in pairs to every town and place where he himself intended to go" (Luke 10:1). The NRSV translation, used throughout this book, states that Jesus appointed *seventy* others because certain early manuscripts feature the number *seventy* instead of *seventy-two*.

It is noted in the NRSV footnote, pertaining to Luke 10:1, that other ancient manuscripts feature the number, *seventy-two*. Consequently, a discrepancy exists over which of the ancient manuscripts feature the accurate number. Did Jesus send out seventy, or did he send out seventy-two? Does it matter?

A close examination of *all* evidence associated with organizational matters suggests that, 72, would be the more accurate number since it represents half of *The Net* of 144. Luke seemed to think it was important to mention this group and their mission. In thinking through the purpose and function of *The Net* of 144, I believe the group of 72 served a valuable purpose, when going out in pairs ahead of Jesus. More will be discussed about the group of 72 in chapter 8 of this book.

The First Believers, Acts 1:15–26

We can be certain that the twelve disciples did not immediately grasp their new role as *fishers of people.* At some point in time, however, they must have realized that Jesus enlisted them to become the first group of 12, in *The Net* of 144. What an honor!

Luke tells us about their early organizational efforts with the following words: "In those days Peter stood up among the believers (together the crowd numbered about 120 persons)" (Acts 1:15). When Luke writes, "In those days," he is referring to the days following Jesus' death, resurrection and ascension. Thus, the crowd of about 120 people reveals the earliest attempt to organize after Jesus' death.

Nevertheless, the group of 120 believers indicates a shortage of people for the first *Net* of 144. Since Luke's gospel reveals the appointment of 72, he must have been aware of the organizational goal, when writing the Acts of the Apostles. The early believers needed 100 people to form a *Net* of 100, plus forty-four additional people to frame *The Net* with two extra loaves of love.

We can be thankful to Luke for including these seemingly minor details—both the number, 72, and the number, 120. It reveals the fact that the disciples were counting heads during the earliest attempts to organize! If they could gather twenty-four additional people, they could complete the first organizational net—the first church of *The Way* of Jesus.

With Peter as the lead fisherman, we can be certain that he was instructing newcomers in the art of net making, but in the midst of the instruction, a problem arose. Peter stood up to address the issue of Judas' betrayal and death. He mentioned that Judas "numbered among us and was allotted his share in this ministry" (Acts1:17). Again, this minor detail reveals that the disciples were organizing a net of believers and, in the process of counting their numbers, they realized how important it was to replace Judas!

If we think about it from their perspective, it makes perfect sense. Since the eleven remaining disciples were recruiting leaders to make a 12 by 12 net, it would have appeared hypocritical if they did not replace one of their own number. Luke mentions that Peter turned to Psalm 109:8 to validate the replacement of Judas. This passage may have been read aloud for the benefit of the new believers who might have questioned why Judas needed to be replaced. Thus, they turned to a fulfillment of sacred text to establish just cause for their decision. We can only imagine the murmurs that may have taken place among the early believers. Let's listen.

> Why is it so important that we count our numbers? Do we *really* need 144 people? Why must there be 12 people in each group? Why aren't 10 people enough? We can build the church with groups of 10s, can't we? *We've always done it that way."*

This imaginary conversation sounds much like the thoughts Christians would have today if presented with the concept of building nets of 144! "Why are the numbers so important? Why can't we just build the church with whomever shows up? *We've always done it that way!* Who cares about numbers! Besides, aren't these number purely symbolic?"

The Literal and the Symbolic

I always thought that most numbers in the Bible are symbolic, representative, or figurative—certainly not anything that would demand a literal adherence. In the first chapter of this book, I mentioned that my research into organizational insights taught me a critical lesson. I'd like to reiterate the importance of the lesson, here.

I assumed that certain numbers were symbolic because the literal reason for their usage escaped me. Today, I write from a different awareness. As I researched the logic and rationale that supported Jethro's use of 1,000s, 100s, 50s and 10s, I began to appreciate the tightness of the ancient organizational fabric. I began to value the solidarity and strength of such an organization.

Most importantly, I saw the portals—gateways, entrances, or large gaps—that would occur in the organizational fabric if even one person chose to disengage. Such holes were made obvious in the previous discussion of the parables of the lost sheep and the lost coin.

I have concluded, therefore, that the numbers, pertaining to organizational matters, are both symbolic *and* literal. They symbolize the organizational image of the church on earth. But they also serve a literal net-making purpose. If the numbers were purely symbolic, Jesus wouldn't have increased the size of the original structure, with four broken pieces of bread, when feeding the crowd of 4,000. If the numbers were purely symbolic, Luke wouldn't have mentioned the group of 72 in his gospel, or the crowd of 120 in the book of Acts. He wouldn't have been concerned with these numbers.

Truthfully, I find no mystical meaning in the numbers. They merely indicate the quantity of people needed for a specific task based on the Ten Commandments, the two laws of love, and the human life cycle from birth to death. Nevertheless, it is entirely possible to build the church of tomorrow with whomever shows up! Christians *have* built the church in this way for many, many centuries.

The more important issue should be our concern with efficiency and effectiveness when we build the church of tomorrow. If Jesus had a specific image in mind for his bride, we should wonder how we can best fulfill *his* vision, rather than grumbling about numbers. If the fulfillment of Jesus' vision requires 144 people per net—and we can *see* the logic that supports the vision—why would we hesitate?

The First Organizational Efforts

Meanwhile, back in the book of Acts, Luke tells us that two men were proposed as replacements for Judas—Joseph, called Barsabbas or Justus, and Matthias. After praying and casting lots, Matthias was chosen, and the eleven disciples became twelve once again. Following the replacement of Judas, Luke's writings move ahead in time to the day of Pentecost. Hence, an unanswered question exists: "Were the disciples able to build their *Net* of 144 by the day of Pentecost?" We will never know. We only know that the disciples were counting people—*in those days.*

While there is no ability to discern how the disciples organized the 120 first believers that had gathered prior to Pentecost, the following illustration offers one possibility. The purpose for including this drawing is to reveal the problem of an *incomplete* organizational attempt. If the church is built with whomever shows up, which of the commandments are sacrificed? If the numbers are ignored, what age groups are neglected? In the example shown below, the elderly are uncared for and the organization is missing one side of its frame of love.

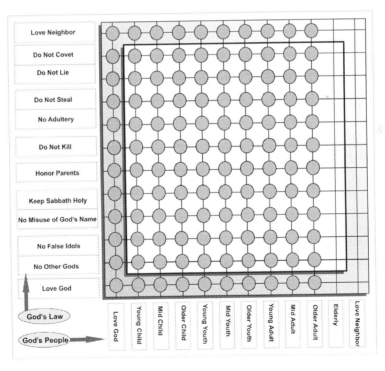

The 120 First Believers

The Church *after* the Church of Acts

The earliest organizational efforts, as recorded in Acts, eventually succumbed to circumstantial problems. The yeast of the religious leaders, Herod, and others, frequently disrupted the believers' attempts to remain organized. Jesus warned the disciples of this possibility. As a result of the disruption, the Christian movement, or *The Way*, was scattered about and persecuted, yet never completely destroyed. Centuries would pass by before the church was encouraged to emerge as an organized body in society.

When she emerged, however, she took on the image of a pyramid, rather than a net. She became the hierarchical institution that has been handed down to us by default. Too much time had passed between the first believers, in the book of Acts, and the emerging church patriarchs, centuries later. The people who walked and talked with Jesus had all died. No one remembered the organizational reasons behind the miracle feedings. Additionally, the book of Revelation, which featured John of Patmos' vision of the church's 12 by 12 image, teetered on the brink of being banned from inclusion in the Bible.

The Net of 144—well hidden within the words of sacred text—was not imagined as the basis for a grassroots movement in Jesus' name. The thought of Christians, standing shoulder to shoulder with all God's people, never took root within the human mind. Christianity quickly became a religion of insiders and outsiders as doctrines of right believing separated the true followers of Jesus from the wrong-believing heretics. In the process of splicing and dicing, *The Net* of 144 simply vanished from spiritual consciousness.

God's Plan A

Much debate has surfaced regarding the number, 144,000, as recorded in the book of Revelation. John of Patmos had two visions pertaining to this number: one of them depicted the sealing of the 144,000, while the other depicted the 144,000 who were with the Lamb.

Some scholars believe that the number simply indicates a large quantity of people, but we must realize that the number was not plucked out of thin air. It symbolizes the image of the church on earth, while simultaneously representing her tightly-woven *Net* of 144 that ministers to 1,000s. It's basic arithmetic—1,000 x 144 = 144,000.

John's Revelation of the 144,000 reveals both the symbolic image of the church triumphant *and* its literal organization of people. But it's important to discern that the change in organization, from 100s to 144s, was always part of God's plan. Even though the increase in size was implemented during Jesus' earthly ministry, it was accounted for much earlier, through the priestly writings in the book of Exodus.

The original tabernacle in the wilderness was constructed with 100 silver bases and 144 gold rings. The 100 bases served as a foundation for the tabernacle, while the 144 rings held the horizontal crossbars that stabilized the sides of the humble, dwelling place. When considered together, the 100 bases and the 144 rings symbolize a *foundation* of Law and an *embrace* of love. As the old covenant of Law was immersed in a new covenant of love, it is important to remember that God's Law remained integral to *both* covenants.

Again, John of Patmos writes, "The city lies foursquare" (Revelation 21:15–17). The city measured 12,000 stadia in length, height and width with walls that were 144 cubits, by human measurement. It's not surprising, therefore, that John describes several different visions of the church: the 144,000, symbolizing the *sealing* of 12,000 in each of the twelve tribes of Israel; the 144,000 and the Lamb, symbolizing Christ's followers who sing a new song; and the Holy City laid out like a 12 by 12 square-shaped cube.

Joyfully, we can say that the 100 silver bases and the 144 gold rings in the ancient pattern of the tabernacle in Exodus, as well as John's visions in Revelation, all point to God's plan A for the church on earth. This is good because I don't think a plan 'B' exists. Since, both Jews and Christians are inescapably related to the image of the church triumphant, should we wonder if it's time to build organizational nets together? We have much in common!

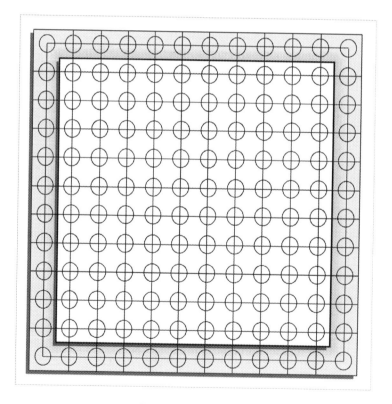

The Square of 144

PART II

The Art of Net Making

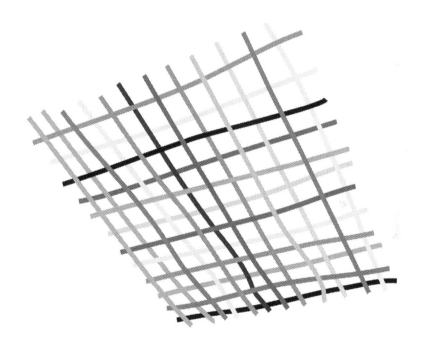

6

When Love Meets Law

Now that we've discovered *The Net* of 100 and *The Net* of 144, we can turn our attention to the art of net making. I've chosen to use the word *art* because net making demands skill, aptitude, and proficiency, which can only come about through continuous practice. It's an art that begins by learning to balance two of the most powerful influences affecting human lives—Law and love.

As illustrated in the opening chapters, *The Net* of 144 consists of intersecting horizontal and vertical lines. The Ten Commandments, as written in Exodus 20, and the laws of love, taken from Deuteronomy 6:4 and Leviticus 19:18, intersect with human life from birth to death. Therefore, this chapter will consider the ways in which love meets Law throughout our lives.

From the Jewish perspective, God's Law is considered to be a supreme blessing. The Law provides a pathway toward a virtuous life, which is something to celebrate! As mentioned earlier, some Christians are under the impression that God's Law was made obsolete through a new covenant in Jesus. Yet the Bible indicates that Jesus did not come to abolish the Law, but to fulfill it.

When the seven loaves of bread were broken, during the feeding of the 4,000, Jesus *sealed* God's Law with love. He dedicated his life to the unpopular mission of inverting the wrongful spirit of arrogance, self-righteousness, and exclusivity that turned God's

Law inside out and upside down. Indeed, Jesus *died* defending a right relationship with God's Law—one that is built on a spirit of love and inclusivity. Thus, Jesus gave his life in order to *fulfill* God's Law of love. This is the good news of Jesus that hasn't received enough attention!

Hopefully, many of the illustrations throughout this book will help Jews and Christians have a better understanding of Jesus' relationship with God's Law. Again, Jesus died defending a right relationship with God's Law and a rightful spirit by which the Law is to be taught, practiced, and preserved. This cannot be overstated.

If the church of tomorrow is to master the art of net making, she must first adopt a healthy relationship with God's Law by wrapping the Ten Commandments in a spirit of love.

The Gift of the Ten Commandments

One way to approach the Ten Commandments is to focus on everything we shouldn't do, or can't do, in order to obey God's Law. Then, when we *do* the things we shouldn't do, we could feel like a worm. A better way to approach the Ten Commandments is to focus on everything we *can* do in order to uphold the Law. Many opportunities arise by turning each of the *do not's* into a command to *do this,* instead. When we succeed in doing something right, we can then celebrate our successes.

The following list, to the right of the Commandments, features the things we *can* do to uphold the Law. Ways in which the Commandments can be wrapped in a spirit of love is provided in the paragraphs below.

God's Law Wrapped in a Covenant of Love

(Exodus 20, paraphrased)

I am God, No Others before Me	*Spiritual Living*
Do Not Create False Idols	*Creative Living*
Do Not Dishonor God's Name	*Respectful Living*
Keep Sabbath Holy	*Restorative Living*
Honor Parents	*Legacy Living*
Do Not Kill	*Nurtured Living*
Do Not Commit Adultery	*Faithful Living*
Do Not Steal	*Honest Living*
Do Not Lie	*Authentic Living*
Do Not Covet	*Contented Living*

I am God. You Shall Have No Others before Me / *Spiritual Living*

People may not agree on who God is, or if God exists, but most people agree that human beings are spiritual creatures. Because each person is created as different as the stars and snowflakes, each soul has a unique relationship with God.

The first commandment suggests that God wants to have an intensely close relationship with the human spirit—in an extremely jealous sort of way! How each person chooses to worship God is a question that each worshipper must answer for themselves. Ideally, worship is a twenty-four/seven way of life. In other words, the life of each person *is* that person's night and day worship of God.

As love meets Law, *The Net* of 144 would encourage people to seek a healthy and productive spiritual life—one that is in a constant state of worship as people go about their daily lives. *The Net* would not dictate when, where, or how a person should worship. Each person in the tribe of 1,000s would be entrusted to develop his or her own unique ways to worship God.

Do Not Create False Idols / *Creative Living*

Imagine a dancer, an ice skater, a painter, or a computer programmer whose innate talents are not welcomed by the church as an act of worship! At one point in time, all of the artists, except musicians, were kicked out of the institutional church for fear that creative thinkers were worshipping their own creativity! We know better now. Even so, we must continue to learn and teach.

Creativity is to be celebrated as the ultimate act of worship, when creativity is used to bring light, joy, hope, and good to society. Creative thinkers, dreamers, and doers, possess the very abilities needed to think outside of the box; color outside of the lines; and transcend the mundane aspects of life in order to change the status quo. When transcending the physical limits of this world, one's mind is open, inspiration is discovered, and the human spirit can co-create with God in the spiritual realm.

When love meets Law, *The Net* of 144 would encourage everyone in her tribe of 1,000s to pursue a healthy and productive creative life—one that turns inspiration into illumination that pleases God and others.

Do Not Take God's Name in Vain / *Respectful Living*

The names of God are many—Yahweh, Jehovah, G-d, God, or Allah, to mention a few. Fulfilling this commandment is as simple as speaking respectfully about God—regardless of the particular name that is used. If we curse God, we curse our own flesh. When love meets Law, *The Net* of 144 would encourage everyone in her tribe of 1,000s to engage in respectful living before God and neighbor—including respectful speaking about God.

Keep the Sabbath Holy / *Restorative Living*

Is the literal day of the week important when it comes to observing Sabbath? Probably not. One's Sabbath could be a Saturday, Sunday, or Thursday. When love meets Law, the focus of this commandment would not be linked to temporal time. The concept associated with the commandment is to engage in restorative living habits. What matters is that we regularly take time to be spiritually, emotionally, psychologically, and physically restored!

People have different ways of finding their restorative paths. For some people, it might be reading a book. For others, it might be fishing. Still others may want to walk around their neighborhood. Some people feel spiritually refreshed by spending time journaling. Others listen to music that may mentally and spiritually transport them to their ideal place of rest. Some people retreat and pray. Whatever restores someone—that is what they must be encouraged to do regularly! When people are rested, they are better able to cope with the daily stresses of life.

When love meets Law, *The Net* of 144 would encourage everyone in her tribe of 1,000s to discover the joy of restorative living and take the necessary time to rest, play, regroup, and restore.

Honor your Father and Mother so that you may live long in the land / *Legacy Living*

It has often been noted that this is the only commandment that is attached to a promise. Honor your elders—live long in the land! In context, the commandment speaks to the children of Israel and their inheritance of the Promised Land.

Unfortunately, it has often been used to put an unhealthy fear of God in children who test boundaries, circumvent rules, or rebel against authority. Such misuse of this commandment can become abusive with lasting emotional and psychological consequences. The deeper essence of this commandment reflects the need for a healthy, parent/child relationship, which in turn, suggests that adult behavior must be worthy of honor.

In its broader sense, the commandment might point to the deeper relationship all humans have with Father Time and Mother Earth. If we honor the creation that sustains us, we will live long in the land that has been given to us. The commandment challenges each generation to participate in the concept of legacy living—both the legacy we leave to our children, as well as the legacy we leave to our earthly nest.

Each member of the tribe of 1,000s will have a legacy to leave. What might that legacy be? Could we leave the world in a better place than we found it? If so, how might we accomplish this? Parents who model this type of thinking would certainly be worthy of their children's honor. When love meets Law, *The Net* of 144 would encourage everyone in her tribe of 1,000s to discover the legacy that has been given to them, and choose the legacy they want to leave to their children!

Do Not Kill / *Nurtured Living*

All life is precious. All life has meaning. All life must be nurtured in order to survive. More importantly, all life must be nurtured in order to *thrive*! Unfortunately, the whole world models immeasurable hypocrisy regarding this commandment! People kill. Societies justify killing in numerous ways! Governments fund killing with money gained through taxpayers—some of whom truly believe that killing people is not in the best interest of anyone.

Aside from physically killing people, a person's spirit can be repeatedly killed with a word, a glance, an attitude, or an unkind gesture, etc. Such killing can lead people into hopelessness and desperation—to the point of suicide or murder.

The commandment says, "Do not kill." To ensure that this commandment isn't broken, human beings must be spiritually and physically nurtured from the moment of birth. It's the only way to stop the killing. When love meets Law, *The Net* of 144 would encourage everyone in her tribe of 1,000s to become *nurturers* for one another.

Do Not Commit Adultery / *Faithful Living*

The literal form of adultery is interpreted as spousal infidelity. In the broader sense, however, this commandment addresses faithful living in all areas of one's life. Living faithfully is nearly impossible if we haven't discerned who we are, as a child of God. What are the spiritual gifts each person has been given? What talent does someone possess? What is one's purpose in life? What is one's passion? What inspires an individual? What can each person contribute to society? How can every person make a difference in their world?

Only when people discover the answers to these questions will they be able to live lives that are faithful to God and neighbor. Far too many people are living adulterated lives because they have not been encouraged to find their God-given reason for living! This lack of discernment produces generations of people who see no reason to be faithful to *anything* or *anyone*. Furthermore, a lack of discernment often causes people to look for an adulterated form of love—in all the *wrong* places.

When love meets Law, *The Net* of 144 would encourage everyone in her tribe of 1,000s to find their God-given passion, purpose, and mission in life; then, faithfully pursue the gifts, passions, and purpose they've discovered.

Do Not Steal / *Honest Living*

This commandment speaks to the issue of taking something that is not rightfully ours to possess. It's about living honestly with one another. Tribal living must be based on honesty, which in turn, builds trust. When trust is built, people unlock their doors, communities come alive, crime decreases, stress declines, and people begin to like where they live.

However, in order to live honestly with one another, we must help people meet their emotional, spiritual, physical, and psychological needs. When needs are not met, people become desperate and they do desperate things. Thus, honest living goes hand in hand with honest *giving* and honest loving. An equitable society produces an honest society. Jesus knew this. It's basic economics. An equitable distribution of bread makes a better society for all! When love meets Law, *The Net* of 144 would encourage everyone in her tribe of 1,000s to live honestly before God and with one another.

Do Not Lie / *Authentic Living*

At some point in time, speaking truth became known as *evangelism*, but the commandment simply says, "Do not lie." The literal interpretation usually focuses on verbal falsehoods. In the broader sense, however, the way to fulfill this commandment is to live *authentically*. In other words, we shouldn't try to be someone we are not.

Instead, we must become the person God designed us to be. That's authentic living in a nutshell. It's the life that I believe God would want every person to demonstrate. Unfortunately, societies have expectations. Sometimes social and cultural rules prohibit a person from living authentically. When that happens, people are forced to lie in order to be accepted in their cultural environment. Yet the commandment says, "Do not lie." When love meets Law, *The Net* of 144 would encourage everyone in her tribe of 1,000s to live authentically before God and with one another.

Do Not Covet / *Contented Living*

Coveting material belongings, achievements, incomes, jobs, or the lifestyles of other people, is a sign of discontentment. When people are content, they need very few possessions to boost their ego. Many pathways toward achieving contentment have been tried. A myriad of suggestions exist in the self-help section of every bookstore, or on popular television talk shows. However, the pathway toward contentment can be summed up by observing the previous nine commandments.

When love meets Law, *The Net* of 144 would encourage everyone in her tribe of 1,000s to discover the kind of contentment that can come through observing God's Law. This can be accomplished by (1) becoming a unique spiritual being (2) discovering one's personal creativity (3) engaging in respectful living (4) enjoying one's Sabbaths

(5) choosing to leave a legacy (6) developing ways to become a nurturer (7) discerning one's purpose in life and being faithful to it (8) living and giving honestly, and (9) living authentically. This is the pathway toward (10) contented living.

Combining Love and Law

The illustration shown below is the most complete image of *The Net* of 144 because it features the spirit of love by which each of the Ten Commandments could be fulfilled.

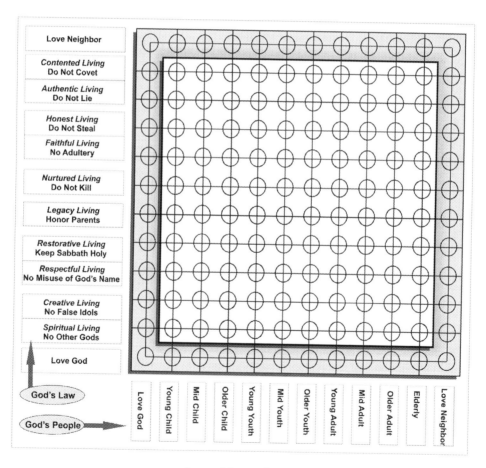

Love Meets Law

God's Law and the Human Lifecycle

When nourishing people with God's Law, it is important to consider the many ways that the Ten Commandments impact people at every stage of the human lifecycle. It's my understanding that the lifecycle, as depicted in *The Net* of 144, is chronological as well as spiritual. *The Net* of 144 would not only minister to the tangible needs of daily life, from birth to death, but it would also nurture spiritual growth among the tribe of 1,000s, from infancy to maturity—a *milk to meat* experience.

During the lifecycle of childhood, God's Law would be digested in its literal sense. For instance, the commandment, "Do not lie," means *do not lie*. As children become teenagers, they would be able to absorb God's Law on a more conceptual level. In this case, the commandment, "Do not lie," translates to the idea of being truthful with God and others. As people become spiritually mature adults, the concept grows inwardly deeper and spreads itself outward. "Do not lie" becomes an ideal. It is a command to live a life that is honest, authentic, and genuine, in order to *become* truth.

As we can see, the relationship between God's Law and the human lifecycle is not a static relationship. God's Law is a living entity that grows and deepens just as people grow and deepen on their journey toward spiritual maturity. Hence, *The Net* of 144 would encourage people to embrace God's Law in different ways according to their chronological age and level of spiritual maturity. The Ten Commandments offer an awesome teaching opportunity at every stage of life!

Bread for the Journey

The responsibility of *The Net* of 144 would be to nourish people with seven loaves of bread, just as Jesus fed the 4,000 before embarking on their homeward journey. This was the ministry of Jesus during his earthly life, and it must ultimately become the ministry of the church of tomorrow. However, the people of God must not lose sight of the fact that the church is experiencing the completion of her own lifecycle—from her infancy in the Sinai Desert, to her image as the church triumphant.

Did she think that her homeward journey would take thousands of years? Perhaps not. Nevertheless, Jesus gave her the bread she needed to sustain her along the way. For her nourishment, on her long-distance journey, Jesus provided the church with seven loaves of bread. Five of the loaves were broken into ten pieces, representing the Ten Commandments. Two of the loaves surrounded the Ten Commandments with love—love of God and love of neighbor. In doing so, Jesus lifted the adolescent church out of the exclusive hands of her Jewish parents; then, set her free in the world. Free to learn. Free to make mistakes. Free to fail. Free to change her ways!

7

Geographic Netting

Another facet of net making is the art of casting, throwing, or spreading nets over a geographic area. *Geographic netting* is a basic concept—not entirely foreign to the institutional church. Local congregations have always sought to serve the needs of local communities. However, the institutional church sought to plant herself in a geographic area, build a house of worship, and call kindred spirits to assemble in the building.

This model of *attraction* satisfied people in the past, but the model has ceased to be effective. It no longer works because it was built on insular thinking that fostered exclusivity. It was built by human beings who had no net-making desires. Therefore, the present institution doesn't look like a net, nor does it model egalitarian thinking or the inclusive teachings of Jesus.

In contrast to this model, *The Net* of 144 would not rely on buildings or call people to assemble in a particular building. Rather, she would cast herself outward as a spiritual covering *over* a specific area. *The Net* would openly disperse spiritual nourishment to a geographic area, instead of keeping the nourishment behind closed doors, through which people must walk, in order to be fed. The difference in vision does not imply that the church of tomorrow won't gather together for worship. The difference only implies that worshiping and serving God does not require a building.

Changing the organizational vision for the church of tomorrow begins by casting a single net in one tiny village, or one little town, or one small neighborhood. This chapter will discuss a big-picture perspective for geographic netting by first looking back in time to an ancient organizational model; then, looking forward in time to a possible future model.

Looking Back in Time

According to the book of Exodus, the original organization of the twelve tribes of Israel were geographically positioned around a relatively small tabernacle. The tribes were arranged in individual camps to the north, south, east, and west of the tabernacle, as mentioned in Numbers 2:1–34. This geographic arrangement established each tribe's location in relationship to the tabernacle.

I mentioned earlier that the Exodus out of Egypt may be mythological rather than historically verifiable. Nevertheless, for the purpose of this discussion, it is only necessary to think about tribal organization as a concept. Whether literal or mythical, the scriptural writings indicate that the tribes were organized geographically.

Purportedly, they were organized in groups of 1,000s, 100s, 50s, and 10s, but the division doesn't begin to convey the vastness of the overall encampment. The book of Numbers records "46,500 young men from the tribe of Reuben who were eligible to serve in the army" (Numbers 1:21). This number does not include the families of these young men. Reuben's entire tribe would have consisted of countless groups of 1,000s, each having their own local nets of 100s, 50s, and 10s.

Including their families, the 46,500 eligible men conveys the enormity of the tribal encampment. And Reuben's tribe was one of eleven other tribes. Even if the encampment is mythological, it reflects a population of millions, which is similar to the population of many major cities around the world today.

The massive geographic encampment of tribes allows us to imagine millions of people who were living, playing, eating, sleeping, giving birth, and dying, while a tiny tabernacle stood silently at the spiritual center of their vast encampment. If we visualize the Holy Place, in the front portion of the tabernacle, we realize that the space could accommodate only a small number of people at one time—perhaps one's immediate family. Thus, the physical structure of this humble dwelling place symbolized the spiritual presence of the divine. It was not the building to which everyone traveled for worship on a Sunday morning. Instead, it represented God's holy *presence* among them.

This is an important concept to think about. Many people erroneously perceive the church as a physical place to which people travel for worship on a Sunday morning—a building made of brick, mortar, or other man-made materials. But the tabernacle of old was not the church! The church, in her infancy, was not the tabernacle. The church was the tribal organization that existed in the vast geographic area *surrounding* the tabernacle! The church was God's *people*—not God's house. The church will forever be God's people!

Looking Forward in Time

The church of tomorrow—if she is to fulfill Jesus' vision for the church triumphant—must begin to see herself as an organization of people who are living, playing, eating, sleeping, giving birth, and dying without a building. Instead of inviting the community to come to a particular place for spiritual nourishment, the church of tomorrow must cast herself out over the spiritual waters and *feed* her people where they are.

The church of tomorrow must believe in her heart that her entire community is the church—not just the people who come to a building, pledge to pay for the dwelling space, and help to maintain the building as it deteriorates. She must see herself as a people of God who live, work, eat, sleep, give birth, and die *together*—in one geographic encampment.

Yes, the church will consist of different tribal [cultural] identities. But she must encourage the sense of *one* encampment. She must see herself feeding people in groups of 1,000s, rather than hoping that a few kindred souls will knock on a physical door and agree to consume a pre-determined brand of spiritual nourishment. Thus, the act of casting, throwing, and spreading nets over a geographic area constitutes a monumental change in perception!

Creating a Spiritual Covering

Geographic netting is comparable to the image of a quilt made of individual squares. If we look at the earth from space, each continent, country, region, city, town, or village, would be covered in organizational squares of leadership—nets of 144. In order to determine the size of a quilt, the population of the town, city, or region must be determined. For instance, if a town has 6,495 households/families, the net makers would round the number to 7,000, in order to cover their town. In this case, a total of seven nets would be needed for their geographic region, or 7 x 1,000.

After determining the number of nets needed, the net makers would then map out smaller geographic areas that each of the seven nets would cover—taking into account the density or scarcity of the population. The seven nets would be cast to the north, south, east, and west of the town. Each geographic section of the town would be covered by 144 residents who live, play, eat, sleep, give birth, and die in their immediate location of 1,000 households.

In the same way, if a city has a population of 780,000, a total of eight hundred nets would be needed to provide an effective spiritual covering for that city. It's a simple equation. If a rural region has a population of 600 residents that are spread out over many miles, that region could be covered by a single net. Care would be taken to determine that the population, covered by *The Net* of 144, is limited to around 1,000 households in order to ensure the best spiritual coverage.

The difference between nets would largely depend on the demographics in each geographic area. Some nets might have a large elderly population and only a small number of children, youth, and young married couples. Other nets might be heavily populated with college students due to a nearby campus. In such cases, colleges and universities may considering casting their own campus nets.

Some nets might have an inmate population to consider if a prison is located in their area, while other nets may have a disabled population to think about. Still other nets could span over rugged mountainous terrain dotted with tiny villages. Regardless of the characteristics of the geographic area, each net would need to become relevant to the unique needs of their tribes of 1,000s.

While every net will have specific concerns, due to the environment in which *The Net* of 144 functions, the overall ministry of every net would be generic in nature. Ministry to, for, and with the tribes of 1,000s is fairly basic. *The Net* simply brings God's Law and God's people together at every stage of the human lifecycle. It is a *comprehensive* approach to ministry, but it's not a *complicated* approach.

Regional Netting

In addition to the spiritual covering for local tribes of 1,000s, geographic netting could include a regional net, or a citywide net, that acts as a central hub for a larger geographic area. The organizational image of the regional net would be identical to that of local nets of 144s. However, the mission and ministry would be different than that of local net.

For instance, citywide nets might be cast for the purpose of teaching the art of net making within the larger region. Such nets might establish a data base of time, talent, and treasure, from which local nets could draw resources. Regional nets might offer traveling professionals who are interested in promoting the netting concept in areas that have no nets. They might offer substitute volunteers who step forward to temporarily fill vacancies in local nets. However, regional or citywide nets would not have any decision-making authority over local nets. They would merely be a supportive presence.

Regional nets may want to establish a central depository through which donated funds, goods, or services could be collected; then, passed from net to net within the region. In such cases, the regional depository might collect grant monies from anonymous donors, and allow those funds to accumulate. Local nets, serving tribes of 1,000s in disadvantaged neighborhoods, could then apply for grants to improve their neighborhoods. The same could be true of monies donated to scholarship funds for various purposes.

Care would need to be taken under these circumstances. The collection of grant monies, or scholarship funds, would need to be transparent to every net in the region. Any distribution of donated funds would need to be approved by every tribe of 1,000s in the region. Since the regional net would have no decision-making authority, it would simply function as a hub for teaching, pooling resources, and depositing funds, goods, or services that ultimately benefit the entire region. The local nets would retain decision-making abilities for their tribes.

Regional or citywide nets could also exist for the purpose of organizing emergency response teams in the event of natural disasters or catastrophic events. Again, a large-area net would have no decision-making authority over local nets or their tribes of 1,000s. When disaster strikes, however, it would be helpful to know that a regional net has been organized and is ready to move people, goods, and services in the event of a disaster.

I recently spoke with a gentlemen who lives in the state of Indiana, USA. During our conversation, he mentioned that he was in dialogue with people who wanted to create a statewide ministry that would benefit the people of their state. He mentioned that the idea centered on gathering people from all of the local churches who were interested in establishing a statewide ministry. His words made me realize that God's Spirit is already moving people in this direction! The only thing missing is an organizational structure!

Again, *The Net* of 144 operates at a grassroots level. Her organizational image stays the same, regardless of the size of the geographic area that *The Net* of 144 serves. Hands on ministry stays with the local net at the local level, where needs are assessed. Fulfilling the Ten Commandments is *The Net's* foundational mission. Ministering to every age in the human lifecycle is also her mission. The only difference between large-area nets and local nets would be the unique goals and objectives of each.

The Role of Spiritual Mentors

Because *The Net* of 144 is a grassroots operation, the role of the pastor, priest, or rabbi, would be much different than that of a pulpit preacher, priest, or rabbi in the institutional church of today. Spiritual mentors, who are called into ministry within a specific geographic region, would be itinerant-minded people who feel comfortable hanging out in coffee shops, lunch counters, soup kitchens, living rooms, hospitals, horse stables, high schools, barber shops, car repair shops, fire stations—anywhere and everywhere.

Such mentors may wish to see themselves as regional advisors who tend to the needs of several tribes of 1,000s. They may want to travel in two's as they visit with people. Some community residents may want to ask the itinerant mentors to conduct a backyard marriage, or baptize a member of their family with water from a nearby pond or lake. They may be asked to confirm someone's faith at a birthday party, or be in attendance when a loved one's ashes are returned to the earth.

The concept may seem foreign to those who have only known institutional tradition. However, this is the work of the church without a building! The itinerant concept simply demonstrates an intimate spiritual presence in the ordinary, yet *extraordinary*, aspects of daily life. This is ultimately one of the goals of geographic netting—to bring the kingdom of God to earth in ordinary, yet *extraordinary* ways.

Reasons to Consider Geographic Netting

The following list provides a few of the benefits of geographic netting.

1. *The Net* of 144 is not built by outsiders. *The Net* is built by the people who live, breathe, work, shop, walk, or drive in their own area! It's a net of the people, by

the people, and for the people. It's a grassroots effort for no other reason than to bring about healing, wholeness, and spiritual health to everyone in their immediate environment of 1,000s.

2. *The Net* of 144 provides a spiritual presence in one's neighborhood, much like *the Presence Bread*—the twelve loaves of bread that were always in God's presence within the ancient tabernacle. (see Holiness Code, Leviticus 24:5–9)

3. *The Net* of 144 does not require membership. Since *The Net* covers a geographic area, she represents every living soul that inhabits the area, so there's nothing to join!

4. *The Net* does not collect money to support herself. *The Net* is strictly an organization of people who wish to ascertain the best quality of life on earth. Any money collected by *The Net* of 144 would benefit the physical and spiritual needs of the entire neighborhood, such as: developing a recreational park, tearing down an abandoned building, setting up a grocery store, restoring an old structure for a youth center, establishing an animal hospital, etc.—anything that might improve the quality of life for the 1,000 residents and their families.

5. *The Net* would break down religious barriers simply because she is a net for all God's people. She would not have a religious affiliation beyond her identity as the kingdom of God. *The Net* would not be theologically divided. She would not be owned or controlled by Presbyterians, Catholics, Jews, Muslims, Pentecostals, Fundamentalists, Episcopalians, Sikhs, or Buddhists, etc. *The Net* of 144 would be all of the above, and none of the above! People would be free to worship God as they please, while simultaneously standing shoulder to shoulder in ministry to their community of 1,000s.

6. *The Net* of 144 would become the link to support services, food banks, clothing banks, exercise groups, day-care providers, mental health clinics, religious

study groups, worship groups, etc. If *The Net* realizes that many youth in the tribe do not have easy access to recreational opportunities; then, the group of 36 people, representing children and teens, would take the necessary action to fill that need. If *The Net* discovers that an elderly man in the tribe does not have transportation to food stores; then, the group of 12 people, representing the elderly, would take action on behalf of that person by linking the man to the services he needs.

7. Because geographical netting serves all people in a given geographic region, it is less likely that needs would go unnoticed. It is less likely that people would fall through societal cracks because those who serve in *The Net* are intimately connected to the 1,000s they serve.

Reality

Obviously, the above description of geographic netting sounds like a new vision for the church of tomorrow. In truth, however, it is an old vision that was never allowed to germinate—an ancient method of tribal survival that was birthed during the Exodus, and later imparted by Jesus during the feeding of the 5,000 and 4,000.

In order for the old vision to become a reality today, the people of God must thirst for it. Good people must hunger for the opportunity to stand shoulder to shoulder for the purpose of healing the world. Trustworthy people who detest dishonest gain, must long for the time when, "the kingdom of heaven is like a net that was thrown into the sea and caught fish of every kind" (Matthew 13:47).

8

Constructing a Net

Now that the idea of spreading nets as a spiritual covering over villages, towns, cities, and regions has been discussed, this chapter will focus on the art of constructing a net. For those who like details, the next few pages will provide the nuts and bolts of net making.

I'll begin by describing the process by which literal fishing nets could be made. Although there are several ways to make a fishing net, I've chosen to focus on the method that ties a net on the ground. While no one needs to know how to make an actual fishing net, the concepts are the same when constructing *The Net* of 144. Hence, it is helpful to have a general understanding of the net-making endeavor.

Net Making on the Ground

When making a fishing net on the ground, the method begins by pounding a stake into the earth, and placing a knotted loop of twine around the stake. From this single knotted loop, which is secured by the stake, the entire fishing net can be tied, knot by knot. As each knot is made, the loops and knots increase in number—from one loop with one knot, to a row of two loops with two knots, followed by a row of three loops with three knots, four, five, and so forth.[2]

As the net grows in size, it becomes *triangular* in shape. When the net is at its desired size, two additional stakes are pounded into the earth to secure the loops at both ends of the longest diagonal row. At this point, the net is secured by three stakes at three corners of the net.

The net maker then begins to decrease the number of loops and knots until only one knotted loop remains, which is placed over a fourth stake in the ground. The overall image of the net is now a *square*. When the completed net is secured to the ground at the four corners of the net, a binding can be knotted or tied around all four sides of the net.

The Four Corners

When considering the function of the four stakes that secure the net at each of its four corners, it seems logical that the art of net making would begin with four people who are willing to ground themselves at the four corners of *The Net* of 144. These four people act as the geographic anchors of *The Net* to the north, south, east, and west of the geographic area to be covered.

Since a fishing net is built with four stakes holding it in position, the net-making process automatically implies that no single individual has ultimate authority over *The Net* of 144. No one preaches to *The Net* of 144. No single person is in charge of spiritual

---

[2] For more information: How to Make Your Own Fishing Net. Visit website, www.britishbushcraftschool.co.uk or video demonstration, https://www.youtube.com/watch?v=qEGjwjrfzGE Published, March 23, 2012. Reference used by permission.

discernment for everyone else in *The Net*. The people who serve at the four corners merely ensure that *The Net* of 144 functions as a ground-level operation.

These four people, who hold *The Net* in place, would logically act as the north, south, east, and west points of contact for the tribe of 1,000s, and *The Net* of 144. In other words, these four individuals would be the ones to call upon when needs or concerns arise within the community. The needs or concerns would then be communicated to the appropriate representatives in *The Net*.

The four people, who anchor *The Net* at its four corners, would logically fulfill the four representative positions of (1) the tribe of 1,000s, (2) *The Net* of 144s, and (3) the two groups of 72s. The people who serve at the four corners of *The Net* might act as spiritual mentors for the tribe of 1,000s, such as pastors, priests, or rabbis, but they could just as easily be trusted lay leaders who live in the area and wish to serve their community in this way. Those who serve in this capacity were mentioned in Jethro's scenario of 1,000s, 100s, and 50s.

The same positions of leadership exist in the increased size of the organization. One person represents the 1,000s. A second person represents the 144s. And two additional people represent the two groups of 72s. The following illustration provides a visual way to imagine the role of these four anchors.

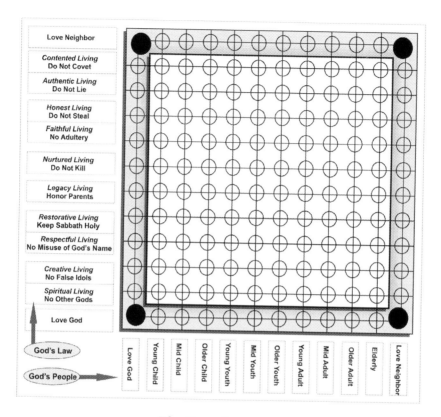

The Four Corners

A Large Sheet with Its Four Corners

Simon Peter, one of the first of the disciples to be called into ministry with Jesus, had a powerful vision of a sheet. Through the words of Luke, Peter's vision of a sheet is described as follows: "Heaven opened and something like a large sheet coming down, being lowered to the ground by its four corners" (Acts 10:11). The entire vision is recorded in Acts 10:11–16, and Acts 11:5–10.

Peter's vision ultimately led him to say, "I truly understand that God shows no partiality, but in every nation anyone who fears him and does what is right is acceptable to him" (Acts 10:34–35). When discussing the spiritual meaning of Peter's vision, our thoughts are usually directed toward the inclusiveness of God's love for humankind. Although the message of inclusiveness is important, I would like to draw attention to the image of a large sheet.

Visual images are important. They convey spiritual truths. In this case, the image is a sheet of fabric, created by weaving horizontal and vertical threads together. By itself, each singular thread in a piece of cloth can easily be broken with a simple tug. When woven together, the resulting fabric is amazingly strong—so strong that it can hold the symbolic four-footed animals, reptiles, and birds of the air, as described in Peter's vision.

The repeated symbolism is staggering. Weaving threads together, to achieve strength, was mentioned at the onset of the organizational discussion. Ten panels of woven cloth were sewn together as a covering over the original tabernacle. The ten panels complement the Ten Commandments and the ten lifecycles in *The Net* of 100—a structure of horizontal and vertical lines. Likewise, the weaving together of horizontal and vertical lines in *The Net* of 144 provides strength for the organization.

Now, in the book of Acts, we are introduced to the image of a sheet being lowered to the ground by its four corners. The fact that the woven cloth was held by *something* at each of its four corners indicates the presence of stability and attachment. In other words, the sheet wasn't floating from the sky in a free-fall manner until it reached the earth. It was intentionally let down, while stabilized at its four corners.

We can deduce that Peter's vision of a large sheet is quite similar to the spiritual image of *The Net* of 144 when stabilized at its four corners. The vision suggests a lowering of a strong, spiritual covering. It draws a mental picture of a square dress for the bride of Christ! We can also conclude that the vision of a sheet, and *The Net* of 144, symbolize inclusive coverings for tribes, communities, and regions—coverings that "show no partiality, but in every nation anyone who fears God, and does what is right, is acceptable to God" (Acts 10:34—35).

A Rotational Method of Operation

Individual nets of 144 would need to determine their own method of operation. The organizational structure itself is not negotiable. *The Net* is what it is! But the method by which the organization chooses to function is extremely flexible! Just as every congregation has its own personality, politics, culture, strengths, and weaknesses— each *Net* of 144 would inevitably be a unique organization of people.

It would be most helpful, however, if *The Net* of 144 would operate with leaders who come and go in rotation. This concept is employed in the traditional church today. Rotational methods would prevent people from adopting an unhealthy sense of ownership of *The Net*. Those who serve in leadership must detest dishonest gain, as mentioned in Exodus 18:21. They must be leaders who have a humble heart, and a desire to promote goodness in their community of 1,000s.

Since *The Net* is driven by its mission to serve communities of 1,000s, it would probably be wise to limit people to a three-year term of service. Rotating leaders anticipates possible fatigue, as well as preempting territorial behaviors within *The Net*. The rotational model could function as follows:

- ○ Year 1: The construction of *The Net* of 144 begins with 72 leaders who agree to spend one year learning about *The Net* and the community it serves; a second year, mentoring 72 new leaders; and a third year, building new nets. During their third year of service, these 72 leaders could fulfill the concept of *sending out the 72*, as recorded in Luke 10. They could go out, in pairs, to help other people establish new nets in new areas.
- ○ Year 2: The construction continues by adding 72 additional leaders who begin their three-year term of service within *The Net*. These 72 leaders are mentored

by the first group of 72 who are serving their second term. *The Net of 144 is now complete.*

- ○ Year 3: The rotation continues with 72 new leaders who begin their three-year term of service by replacing the first group of 72 who have been *sent out*. This new group of 72 are mentored by the second group of 72 who are serving their second term of service.

- ○ Year 4: The rotation continues with 72 new leaders who replace the second group of 72 who have been *sent out* to help build new nets in another geographic location.

By employing this rotational method of operation, *The Net* of 144 would be complete in a two-year period of time. *The Net* would become fertile in three-years, as 72 people are sent out to help establish new nets for other tribes of 1,000s. Eventually, an entire geographic region would be covered with nets of 144. Once an area is fully netted, the length of service, within the original net that initiated the covering, could be reduced, from a three-year term to a two-year rotation. If *The Net* is successful in its mission, former leaders will most likely want to volunteer for additional rotations *after* they have taken time for restoration and retreat.

A Nonprofit Volunteer Effort

Since *The Net* of 144 is cast out over a geographic area, *the church becomes the tribe of 1,000s* that is covered by *The Net*. The church *is* the tribe, and the tribe *is* the church. This implies that the tribe of 1,000s reaps the benefit of the work it initiates through its own volunteers who rotate in and out of *The Net*. The goal of *The Net*, therefore, is not to capture people *for* the kingdom of God, but to set people free *within* the kingdom of God.

The Net of 144 would never say to its geographic tribe of 1,000s, "You can be part of our net if you *do* this, *believe* that, *profess* what we profess, and *confirm* what we confirm . . ." No! Instead, *The Net* would say, "You are part of a net of 1,000s. An organized group of 144 people—representing all ages, races, cultures, religions, creeds, and ethnicities—has been created to help our tribe enjoy the best possible life within our location on earth." In other words, *The Net* of 144 would not ask the neighborhood to come to God's kingdom. *The Net* would declare that the kingdom of God is at hand—*living in everyone*—without exception.

Since *The Net* of 144 is not concerned with purchasing property or constructing buildings, she is free to concentrate solely on the mission of bringing hope and healing to her community. Her volunteer foundation would gather resources from her tribe of 1,000s in order to care for the needs of 1,000s. When time, money, or donated goods are collected from the tribe of 1,000s, those resources would be given back into the tribe of 1,000 in order to directly benefit the tribe.

For instance, if the tribe does not have safe recreational spaces where children and youth can meet, play, and enjoy the companionship of their peers, the entire tribe could offer their resources to create such places. The donated resources might be in the form of submitting ideas, developing plans, donating a gift of property, offering time, money, construction, remodeling, maintenance, etc. *The Net* would not be responsible for supplying the tribe with safe recreational spaces. The tribe would need to supply itself with play spaces. And the tribe would need to maintain such areas!

If the community of 1,000s has a significant elderly population that needs transportation to and from doctor appointments, the entire tribe might wish to establish a medical mission team that shuttles people from place to place. This service could provide employment for a few people in the tribe, while offering a much needed service to its older residents. *The Net* of 144 might want to estimate the cost of operating the shuttle, hours of operation, drivers, salary, and number of residents needing the service.

The Net of community leaders would then propose the idea to the tribe of 1,000s and ask for financial support for the service. Once the necessary resources are obtained, the service could be launched. Again, *The Net* of 144 would not supply the service for the community of 1,000s. The community would need to provide the service for itself, along with sustaining the service.

The same would be true of food pantries, day-care services, hair-cutting services, or car-repair services. The ideas are endless, but the mission is to elevate the quality of life for all who live, play, eat, sleep, give birth, and die, in a certain geographic area.

Hopefully at this point in the discussion, the construction and function of *The Net* of 144 is beginning to make sense. Every trustworthy person would have an opportunity to represent the kingdom of God for their neighborhood of 1,000s. If *The Net* is successful in her endeavors, she will fulfill her mission of empowering people for the collective good of society.

Once a net is built, the key to *The Net's* success could be summed up by her

- Desire to stay humble and emit love.
- Yearning to win the trust of her tribe.
- Patience when listening to the concerns of others.
- Focus on accepting people wherever they are in their spiritual journey.
- Ability to act on behalf of the needs of her people.
- Willingness to be creative in problem solving
- Commitment to attain the highest possible quality of life for all people

This has always been the intention of the traditional church, but *The Net* of 144 would accomplish such goals without (1) the expense of physical buildings (2) proselytizing (3) purchasing pricy educational materials (4) developing church programs (5) staffing such programs, and (6) monetarily supporting such programs. Volunteers would focus 100% of their time and energy bringing God's Law and God's people together in order to achieve the best possible life in a specific geographic region.

The ratio of leaders who serve in *The Net* of 144 is roughly 15% of the population of 1,000s. That's a relatively small percent of the overall population of each tribe of 1,000s. It is likely that the percentage of people who believe in God, and respect God's Law, is far greater than 15% in most geographic areas. Consequently, it *would not be impossible* for net makers to inspire 15% of the population to build a net for their immediate community.

Appointing Representatives of 12s

The four people, who anchor *The Net* at its four corners, would logically be the four representatives of the tribe of 1,000s, *The Net* of 144s, and the two groups of 72s. As mentioned above, these four people speak for the population in the northern, southern, eastern and western quadrants of the community of 1,000s.

Within *The Net*, however, twenty additional representatives would be appointed to ease the flow of communication within the smaller groups of 12s. For instance, each group of 12 may wish to appoint a contact person to represent their group during the two or three-year term of service—twenty contacts in all. These people reflect Jethro's suggestion to appoint a representative for the smallest groups of 10s. When Jesus added the two laws of love, the smallest groups added two people to become a group of 12.

The appointed representatives of 12s would not have any additional decision-making power in *The Net*. They would simply agree to speak on behalf of their group, and act as the contact person for their team of 12. In this way, the egalitarian nature of *The Net* is upheld, and communication flows as easily as possible.

Two Teams

Everyone who serves as a leader in *The Net* of 144 agrees to focus on one age group, in the human lifecycle, and one of the commandments. Every leader in *The Net* has a dual focus because the leader serves on two teams of 12 people on each team. Everyone on the two teams of 12 has an equal voice in decision making because every voice speaks from a different perspective—one age group and one commandment per leader.

With everyone in *The Net* of 144, serving on two teams of 12 members each, it's easy to see that *The Net* is truly a 12 by 12 operation. Every person serves on a team with eleven other people, who are focused on the same lifecycle, but from the perspective of a *different commandment*. Every person serves on a team with eleven other people, who are focused on the same commandment, but from the perspective of a *different lifecycle*. Hence, *every voice* is necessary!

Within the two teams of 12, four leaders provide a continuous supply of spiritual nourishment to both teams, as shown in the illustration below. These four individuals agree to serve as the four-sided binding of *The Net*. Their role is to constantly nourish the organization with the bread of love, uphold the covenant of love, and ensure that the organization remains true to its rightful spirit of love.

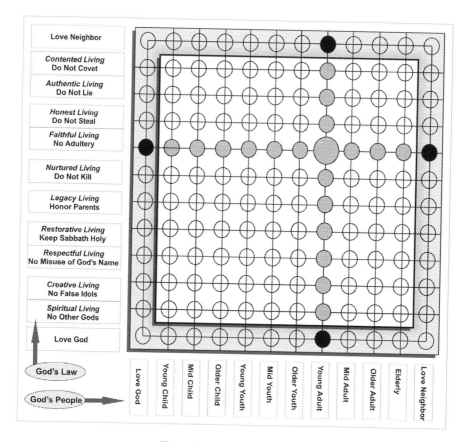

Two Teams of Twelve

Rings, Knots and Crosses

Communicating the net-making vision will be challenging to say the least. It's difficult to change people's perceptions. However, understanding the depth of spirituality that undergirds *The Net* of 144 may be the key to its acceptance.

Ordinary people hold *The Net* of 144 together just like the 144 gold rings that held the ancient tabernacle together. Spiritually speaking, it could be said that each of the 144 people who serve in *The Net*, is an embellishment on the church's bridal dress. This is her adornment, as she reflects the image of a bride who is dressed for her husband, in Revelation 21:1–2.

Those who volunteer to represent their community of 1,000s may also want to learn about the original tabernacle and its spiritual presence for the tribes of 1,000s, 100s, 50s, and 10s. Such insight would naturally connect God's people to the richness of their spiritual heritage, when volunteering to serve within *The Net*—a legacy that was first passed to Jesus; then, to us.

The people who serve in *The Net* would also symbolize the 144 knots that tie *The Net* together. The knots could be thought of as embroidery on the church's bridal dress. The knots are located at the intersection of each vertical and horizontal line in *The Net*. When each person chooses to represent a specific age group and a specific commandment, their focus on that particular aspect of ministry ties the knot at that intersection. Thus, every knot in *The Net* ties God's Law to God's people. A well-tied net is critical to the overall success of *The Net*.

Additionally, each intersection within *The Net* of 144 is in the image of a cross. All things considered, the 144 net makers hold three privileged positions as follows: (1)

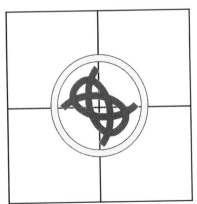
Rings, Knots, and Crosses

they represent one of the 144 gold rings that held the ancient tabernacle together (2) they represent one of the 144 knots that secure God's Law to God's people, and (3) they take up 144 crosses in remembrance of the tabernacle of old or in remembrance of Christ. For Jews and Christians who understand the spiritual symbolism of *The Net*, these concepts would be exceptionally meaningful.

Grounded without a Building

Once constructed, *The Net* of 144 would never be seen as a static entity. People aren't static by nature. Each *Net* would function as a living entity within a community of living souls. *The Net* would not resemble a congregation of 144 people who come together, build a building, and operate from within its walls. In fact, it would be desirable if *The Net* of 144 never owned physical property, as previously mentioned.

If she is to be perceived as a spiritually free organization, *The Net* of 144 would need to reveal herself as a nomadic entity within her community. Like the earthly ministry of Jesus, *The Net* would not have, *or need*, a place to lay her head. She would perform her mission without a physical roof to cover her, walls to protect her, or doors that must be opened in order to approach her. Instead, *The Net* of 144 would *provide* a spiritual covering, *offer* spiritual protection, and *become* the door for 1,000s.

9

Preparing for the Church of Tomorrow

The church has always lived in the heads, hands, and hearts of the people of God. She was born to the people of Israel, and set free through the life and teachings of Jesus. She is currently on her way to becoming the bride of Christ at the end of the age.

Several factors could determine the church's spiritual readiness to embark on a net-making adventure in villages, towns, and cities. One factor is spiritual maturity. Another is God's timing. I believe the church's readiness depends on both factors. Therefore, this last chapter examines some of the signs that might indicate a state of readiness.

A Desire for Inclusiveness

The church universal has spent the past 2,000 years examining every drop of water within her spiritual body. She did so, in an attempt to define God, Jesus, and Spirit, with human words. But something unexpected happened in the process of creating definitions. As the church exercised her theological muscles, she split herself apart into hundreds of differing perspectives—each one claiming to be better than the previous.

The church discovered something in her attempt to clarify who she was and what she stood for: *it isn't possible to define God, nor should we try!* God cannot be captured, confined, or limited to human thought. Therefore, a sure sign of net-making readiness will be a thirst for inclusivity. This will happen as the church spends less time defining her beliefs about God, and more time loving God's people, regardless of their beliefs.

Slowly but surely, people are accepting ideas, beliefs, opinions, philosophies, and theologies that differ from their own perspective. Friends are listening to each other and learning from each other. Diversity will always exist, but the church of tomorrow will thrive on it! She will enjoy the beauty of diversity as one who marvels at the myriad of stars in the night sky.

Attentiveness to Spiritual Autonomy

A full embrace of spiritual autonomy will be another sign that the church is ready to build nets. The church must be willing to give up her need to control the spiritual thoughts of God's people. If she has any hope of winning back those who have walked away from her institutional image, she must curb her need to preach on and on—like Paul, who couldn't stop talking at midnight when bidding farewell to the people of Troas, Acts 20:7–12. If the church continues to preach *to* and *at* people, she should expect many young souls, like Eutychus, to fall asleep in her presence; then, tumble out of windows to their deaths.

Over the centuries, the traditional church has been guilty of stifling spiritual discernment, creativity, and imagination—the very thought processes needed to nurture healthy listening skills in the spiritual realm of communication. Much stifling occurs because the church promotes the idea that spiritual discernment is best left to professional leaders, such as rabbis, pastors, priests, nuns, bishops, or educators, who are deemed qualified to interpret sacred text for others.

When people are told what to believe—and why they should believe it—spiritual discernment becomes something that is done *for* them instead of *by* them. When answers are provided for questions that have yet to be asked—why ask them? Under these circumstances, the gift of discernment isn't needed, creative thinking isn't fostered, and imagination dies of dehydration.

If told what to drink, people do not learn how to obtain *living water* for themselves. While telling others what to believe may be well-intentioned, it most definitively numbs spiritual inquiry. When muscles aren't exercised, they atrophy. The same is true with spiritual discernment. We either use it or lose it. If we do not exercise this innate ability, we quickly become spiritually sleepy. Worse yet, we become parrots that can only mimic the repeated words taught by keepers.

The gift of spiritual discernment is not exclusive to those who have embarked on a lifelong career in theological study. God's Holy Spirit moves within the mind and heart of anyone who asks, seeks, and knocks. God's Spirit is capable of speaking to people who have an in-depth knowledge of the Bible, or no working knowledge of it at all! In ancient times, God spoke to people through images of light, color, and nature. God still speaks through nature, today. God also speaks to people through pleasant surprises, or unwelcomed circumstances that have impacted their lives.

People don't need the answers that others have found. They need permission to ask their own questions and embark on their own quest for answers—those that make sense inside their own soul. The power to discern one's own spiritual beliefs, and govern one's own spiritual life, creates a relationship with God that is both *personal* and *autonomous!*

When the church is ready to build nets, she will also be ready to allow the wind of God's Spirit to blow where it may. When permission is freely given, the gifts of discernment, creative thinking, and human imagination will grow. Living water will flow and spiritual autonomy will flourish.

A Commitment to Stand Shoulder to Shoulder

The church will know that she is ready to build nets when she recognizes the good that can come from standing shoulder to shoulder with people who think and believe differently from each other. When the ultimate goal is to achieve peace and harmony in one's community, it really doesn't matter what people believe. The goal is peace and harmony. We are moving in this direction, but we have a long way to go in order to master the concept.

In order to reach this idealistic place of spiritual readiness, God's people must rely less on the language of human words—especially those that parse, categorize, and label. Instead, we must rely more heavily on the common tongue that is spoken by and through the Creation—our earthly nest. The church will also know that she is ready when she hears God's Spirit "changing the speech of peoples, that all may call on God and serve him with one accord" (Zephaniah 3:9). That day lies ahead of us.

A Willingness to Share Illumination without Indoctrination

Lastly, the church's readiness will be marked by her willingness to share illumination regardless of circumstances. In order to discuss this final topic, it may be helpful to examine the parable of the wise and foolish maidens.

The obvious message in this well-known parable is spiritual preparedness. However, we know that Jesus' parables are never as simple as the observable message implies. The stories are layered and complex. They contain less obvious levels, which pose puzzling riddles that can only be solved by the person who dares to dig deeper. In this case, we must discover the veiled message of *spiritual immaturity* in the parable of the young maidens; then, desire its inverse—*spiritual maturity*.

The Parable of the Ten Young Maidens

The parable of the ten young maidens, Matthew 25:1–13, paints a rather bleak picture of the future church at midnight. The parable is told from Jesus' perspective 2,000 years ago. We know that Jesus was projecting a future scenario of the church because the parable begins with the words, "*Then* the kingdom of heaven *will be* like this" (Matthew 25:1).

Then is the projected time of midnight. The apex of the parable occurs when a midnight cry rings out. Midnight is when the ten sleeping maidens wake up! Midnight brings about a spiritual shift from sleepiness to alertness. The shift occurs when an announcement is made, "Look! Here is the bridegroom! Come out to meet him!" (Matthew 25:6).

It is critical that we see the hour of midnight as a spiritual turning point! I've mentioned three midnight hour references in this book, thus far: (1) the sailors took soundings and dropped anchor at midnight in Acts 27, (2) Eutychus fell to his death as Paul preached on and on at midnight, in Acts 20, and (3) the sleepy maidens wake up, in Matthew 25. The Bible contains a total of twelve midnight-hour turning points. Six references appear in the Hebrew Bible. Six references appear in the New Testament.

The midnight-hour turning point, in Matthew 25, provides an opportunity to ask, "Do we like the picture that Jesus paints of the church at midnight?" If we don't like the picture, do we have the power to change it? Do we have the power to take soundings, drop anchor, and prepare to abort our ship? Do we have the power to stop preaching on and on about Jesus, and start employing the talents of people who might otherwise fall asleep in our midst? Do we have the power to discern a midnight-hour cry and wake up? Yes! I believe we have the power.

Problematic Thinking

Jesus develops the parable of the church at midnight with a total of 10 young maidens— the smallest numeric grouping in *The Net* of 1000s, 100s, 50s, and 10s. Hence, Jesus presents another parable that mentions groups of 10s. Having said that, Jesus states that the maidens are divided into two groups of five maidens each. Five maidens reflect an *incomplete* grouping in the organizational structure of 1,000s, 100s, 50s, and 10s. Something is wrong with this picture!

Division is the first of many problems in this parable. If we consider the organizational factor, we can immediately discern the division. The separation implies that the maidens were not acting in the best interest of the whole. It suggests that the young maidens split apart into separate groups that were thinking and working toward their own end. It suggests that the ten young maidens were not holding each other accountable in a spirit of love. They didn't *have each other's backs*, as the saying goes.

Sadly, Jesus' story is an accurate depiction of the church of today—an entity of divided maidens who are thinking and working toward their own end. The Christian church in particular has splintered herself into numerous sectors including: Presbyterian's, Lutheran's, Episcopalian's, Catholic's, Baptist's, Methodist's, Mennonite's, Fundamentalist's, Non-Denominationalist's, Pentecostal's, Progressive's, Conservative's, Evangelical's, and many more—each working independently and hesitant to work collectively. The Muslim and Jewish traditions are also divided.

Labeling is the second problem. If we know anything about Jesus, we know that he did not approve of labels. He spent his entire ministry trying to dissolve them. Therefore, the contrasting labels that Jesus applied to the young maidens should alert us to a spiritual puzzle. One group is given the *foolish* label and the other group is given the *wise* label. The labels pose a challenging conundrum.

Sure enough, we learn that the young maidens act according to their respective labels. The foolish maidens don't think to take extra oil with them when they embark on their journey to meet the bridegroom, whereas the wise maidens planned ahead. Of course they did! They were the wise ones!

Again, this is the picture of the church, today. Each of the names given to our divisions, such as Baptist, atheist, Catholic, Jew, or agnostic, are labels that separate people, one from another. Of the many labels listed above—which maidens are wise? Which ones are foolish? Many Christians would be delighted to offer their opinions.

Sleepiness is yet another problem. Neither group of five maidens expected the bridegroom to take so long in coming. Hence, both groups fell asleep. How wise was that! Wasn't it rather foolish? Nevertheless, when the midnight cry rang out, "Look! Here's the bridegroom! Come out to meet him," the ten maidens woke up and trimmed their lamps. That's when panic strikes!

Fear becomes the next problem. This human emotion marks the point where the parable takes a more troubling turn. When the foolish maidens realized that they didn't have enough oil, they asked the wise maidens for help. But the wise maidens feared a shortage of oil, so they refused to share what they had! Instead of sharing, the wise maidens told the foolish maidens to go find oil for themselves!

Sending people away is another problem. Remember that it's midnight, but the wise maidens do not hesitate to send the foolish maidens away from the only available light. "Go out into the dark of night and buy some oil from the merchants who sell it. Good luck! I hope you make it." Doesn't this story sound oddly familiar? Prior to the feeding of the 5,000, didn't the disciples ask Jesus to send the shepherd-less crowd away to buy bread for themselves? Yes! And we should be bothered by a repeated pattern of sending people away to fend for themselves in a world of buyers and sellers.

The Consequences of Problematic Thinking

This parable is not a simple story of wise people who were ready to meet the bridegroom, or foolish people who weren't prepared. At greater depths, this parable reveals a disorganized nightmare! It paints a pitiful portrayal of spiritual immaturity at midnight—a recipe for societal disaster.

When the wise, young maidens, with their well-lit lamps, arrive at the wedding banquet—the door is shut. When the foolish maidens return to the scene, they ask, "Lord! Lord! Open to us!" The bridegroom replies, "Truly I tell you, I don't know you" (Matthew 25:11–12). Notice that Jesus does not mention whether the foolish maidens ever found any oil after traipsing out into the darkness. He simply reveals that the bridegroom doesn't recognize them. Obviously they didn't find illumination!

Are we satisfied with the consequences that play out in this parable? Doesn't the story display the epitome of self-centeredness—every maiden for herself! Shouldn't the attitude of the wise maidens concern us? Shouldn't this parable cause us to wonder where the wise maidens obtained their wisdom! Who was their teacher?

If the wise maidens were truly wise, wouldn't they have said to their sisters, "Have faith! We have plenty of oil! Come. Let's walk to the banquet together." Why did the wise maidens think that they would run out of oil? Didn't they trust the eternal source of their illumination? Were they burning human energy in their lamps? If they had an extra measure of oil, why didn't they have compassion for their spiritual sisters who fell asleep next to them? Were they secretly holding a permanent grudge over a past division? Why didn't they know that illumination cannot be purchased from a merchant?

What about the foolish maidens! In addition to the fact that they didn't plan ahead, why did they trust the wisdom of the wise maidens? Why did they leave the only available light and wander into the dark of night to buy oil that can't be purchased? Is that not the perfect example of the blind being led by the blind? Nevertheless, off they went.

Imagining Spiritual Maturity

Wouldn't it be better to imagine a different midnight-hour ending to this parable? I think so! Nothing can be done about the division that exists between the maidens prior to midnight. The division is what it is. Jesus disclosed it. Likewise, nothing can be done about sleepiness prior to midnight. Jesus revealed it. Even so, everything can change in this parable once the maidens wake up from their slumber. But a different ending requires radical change at midnight.

As mentioned earlier, midnight indicates a critical turning point from sleepiness to alertness in this parable. It marks a spiritual shift by the mere fact that the maidens wake up! If we don't like the way things play out in this parable; then, it's up to us (all God's people) to wake up—whether we perceive a midnight cry, or not. From the midnight hour forward, Jesus illuminates the *choices* made by the young maidens— choices that are *changeable*!

Midnight is *not* the end of this story! Midnight is the *beginning* of the church's journey toward the banquet room where a wedding will eventually take place! Every aspect of Jesus' parable can be changed from the moment that the maidens wake up, to the moment that the door is shut!

Jesus does not disclose the length of time that passes between hearing the midnight cry and entering the banquet room. It could be a long, long time. Christians must realize that the church's journey, from the midnight hour to the banquet room, could take another 2,000 years! That being said, it is well within the church's power to wake up, right now, and change her ways.

Personally, I believe an unspoken opportunity for change lies at the heart of this parable. I believe Jesus offered this pitiful picture of the future church at midnight, in an attempt to give her the gift of time! Time to think and time to mature. Time to change her dress. Time to become the woman Jesus envisioned for his spiritual bride.

An alternative ending to the parable would begin with ten young maidens who

- Realize the importance of working together in spirit.
- Hold each other accountable in love.
- Drop labels for the sake of unity.
- Share wisdom.
- Realize that their eternal source of illumination cannot be purchased.
- Understand that spiritual illumination is a free gift.
- Encourage each other to trust that their light will never run out!
- Keep each other awake and alert in the spiritual sense.
- Agree that watchfulness is everyone's job, for no one knows the day or hour.

This is a depiction of spiritual maturity. It is a picture that ensures plenty of illumination for everyone when the midnight cry is heard, and enough illumination for everyone to make their way to the banquet table *before* the door is shut.

As the people of God move into the church of tomorrow, we must ask ourselves whether we are spiritually mature enough to join hands with all God's people in an organized, shoulder to shoulder effort, that brings a greater degree of illumination to every community on earth. We must question whether the church of today is ready to hear the words, "Look! Here's the bridegroom! Come out to meet him?" If she isn't ready to unselfishly respond to these words; then, what changes must the church of today implement, in order to say, "We are wide-awake and ready."

10

The Work of the Church of Tomorrow

Jesus said, "The kingdom of heaven is like a net" (Matthew 13:47). Like the parable of the wise and foolish maidens, I believe Jesus told the parable of the net for the purpose of informing the church as she matures. I believe that Jesus wanted to provide the church with the organizational image he had in mind for his bride—knowing full-well that she would need to be reminded of the image of a net someday.

This particular parable also offers the church an ordered sequence of tasks that she is to undertake, at appointed times, during her homeward journey. In my opinion, the parable of the net embodies the work of the church as Jesus envisioned it happening over time.

> "Again, the kingdom of heaven is like a net that was thrown into the sea and caught fish of every kind; when it was full, they [fishermen] drew it to shore, sat down, and put the good into baskets but threw out the bad. So it will be at the end of the age. The angels will come out and separate the evil from the righteous" (Matthew 13:47–49).

Discerning Order and the Passage of Time

We may not think about the passage of time when we read the parable of the net, but we should. The sequence of events within the parable transpires over a period of time. Although the duration of time is undisclosed, the words offer a sequential order of tasks that Christians must consider! Discerning an accurate progression of activity over time, is critical to the church's success in mission. The activity is as follows:

1. Throw a net into the sea.
2. Catch fish of every kind.
3. When the net is full, pull it to shore.
4. Sit down.
5. Collect good fish and put them in a basket.

The traditional church has been engaged in a fishing expedition for 2,000 years, yet by her own admission, she hasn't discerned that her net is full. This is an important realization. The church gleefully announces that there is room for all! Such statements suggest that the church is attempting to complete the first and second tasks in the list above. She is trying to fill her net and it isn't full, yet! Discerning a full net is the third task. So, we can conclude with certainty that the church is currently working on the first and second tasks.

I think it's also fair to say that the church is perceived to be a collector of good fish for God's basket. However, that's step five on the church's 'to do' list! Putting fish in God's basket is to be accomplished only *after* the church's net is full and pulled to shore!

Can we *see* the church's problem when discerning her order of business? From all indications, it seems that the sequential order of tasks has been violated because the church has not yet completed the first and second tasks. Engaging in the fifth task, before the first and second tasks have been completed, suggests that the church has jumped ahead of herself. She is trying to complete a task that has not yet reached its appointed time.

Violating the sequential order of tasks in Jesus' parable indicates the reason for so much spiritual confusion! That's what happens when people surge ahead of God. To engage in an activity, *before* determining a ripeness of time, is a sure sign of too much human control.

This realization does not imply that blessings have not occurred in spite of the church's lack of discernment. I believe that God faithfully sanctifies human efforts that are born of good intentions, because God knows good people are not perfect people. Nevertheless, confusion over the sequential order of her tasks is one reason that a transfiguration of the church is necessary at this point in time.

The Right Side of the Boat

In addition to violating a sequential order of tasks, it is quite possible that the traditional church has been fishing on the left side of her boat for the past 2,000 years. According to the following account, the miraculous catch will only occur if our nets are thrown on the *right side* of the boat.

> After these things Jesus showed himself again to the disciples by the Sea of Tiberias; and he showed himself in this way. Gathered there together were Simon Peter, Thomas called the Twin, Nathanael of Cana in Galilee,

the sons of Zebedee, and two others of his disciples. Simon Peter said to them, "I am going fishing." They said to him, "We will go with you." They went out and got into the boat, but that night they caught nothing. Just after daybreak, Jesus stood on the beach, but the disciples did not know that it was Jesus. Jesus said to them, "Children, you have no fish, have you?" They answered him, "No." He said to them "Cast the net to the right side of the boat, and you will find some" (John 21:1–6a).

I see the distinction between *left* and *right* as a difference in brain function! Obviously, our present knowledge of the human brain was unknown when this account was written. But the knowledge gives us the necessary vocabulary to describe the disciples' change in perception.

One who fishes on the left side of the boat concretely thinks, "My job is to *catch* fish." The left-sided fisherperson fails to capture the thrill of fishing because one's focus is on the end result of obtaining objects, or *winning souls* for Jesus.

One who fishes on the right side of the boat conceptually thinks, "My job is to *cast* a net." The right-sided fisherperson takes delight in fishing because the thrill is in mastering the art of throwing one's net out over the water! In this scenario, the movement of God's Spirit fills the net. Winning souls for Jesus is not the goal.

John mentions that the disciples didn't recognize Jesus as they fulfilled his request. So, we can deduce that the miraculous catch was not the result of recognizing Jesus. Rather, the disciples' attention shifted from capturing fish, to throwing a net. And a miracle occurred in the process. The church must learn the difference between the two sides of the boat.

Eventually, the church's net *will* be full, and God's people will know beyond a shadow of doubt that the end of the age has come. *At that time,* she can pull her net to shore and present her catch to the angels who are patiently waiting to collect the good fish for God's basket.

Until then, I believe that the church's work must change from catching fish *for* the kingdom of heaven, to the art of making, throwing, and spreading nets that *bring* the kingdom of heaven to the fish. In doing so, Jesus' vision for his bride will be realized, and her image will reflect the description of the New Jerusalem. Likewise, she will fulfill Ezekiel's vision of a river flowing from a new temple into a life-giving creation.

> "People will stand fishing beside the sea;
>
> from En-gedi to En-eglaim;
>
> it will be a place for the spreading of nets;
>
> its fish will be of a great many kinds,
>
> like the fish of the Great Sea"
>
> —Ezekiel 47:10

Epilogue

Time Will Tell

My journey into the subject of organization began with a vision of a grid that unexpectedly appeared before my eyes on October 18, 1996. I did not ask to see the image. Moreover, I didn't understand why the vision was shown to *me*. I lack the typical credentials that would qualify me as a person with organizational skills and expertise. Nevertheless, I couldn't forget what I saw, or what I learned.

As I prayed for guidance and waited for direction, the vision not only grew in size, but also in spiritual depth. What started out to be a simple organizational tool for ministry, ultimately became a structure that is deeply rooted in the words of sacred text.

After realizing that *The Net* was well hidden in the words of the Bible, I was even more puzzled as to why the image had become visible to me. I became comfortable with the image of *The Net* only after understanding it to be *Jesus'* vision for the church—not *my* vision for the church! In other words, I was finally able to discern that I was to act as a *messenger*—a role I could handle!

I mentioned, in the introduction, that the information is an offering of seeds to be planted in the garden of human imagination. In the opening chapter, I put forth the notion that the church is in the process of a transfiguration that would radically change the outward appearance of the bride of Christ. I imparted scriptural evidence, from which *The Net* of 100 emerges, as well as *The Net* of 144. I laid out an organizational vision for the church of tomorrow that is, in many ways, an inversion of the institutional church, and how it presently functions.

Not in my wildest imaginings would I expect the vision of *The Net* and its geographic covering to be immediately embraced by God's people. The day when net makers emerge, build the first nets, and cast them out over the spiritual waters of villages, towns, or cities may be a long time in coming—long after my death, I suspect. In the meantime, spiritual gardens must be tilled. Seeds must be planted, and soil must be fertilized. The germination of ideas takes time.

That being said, I do expect that the people of God will eventually be led, by the wind of God's Spirit, to consider the art of net making as a viable option for carrying out effective ministry. In light of the evidence collected from the Bible, I make the claim that *The Net* of 144 is the image of "the New Jerusalem, coming down out of heaven from God, prepared as a bride adorned for her husband" (Revelation 21:2). I also conclude that the foursquare image, described as "the bride, the wife of the Lamb" (Revelation 21:9), is a vision of the same organizational image that was

- Captured by Jethro and implemented by Moses in Exodus 18:21, 25.
- Nourished by Jesus during the feeding of the 5,000 in Mark 6:30–44.
- Framed with two loaves of love during the feeding of the 4,000 in Mark 8:1–9.
- Referenced in the parables of a lost sheep and a lost coin in Luke 15:3–10.
- Adopted by the first 120 believers in Acts 1:15.
- Appeared to Simon Peter as a large sheet in Acts 10 and 11.
- Envisioned by John of Patmos in Revelation 7, 14, and 21.

In the prologue I suggested that the institutional church is undergoing a transfiguration which will change the outward appearance of the church universal. I also suggested that the violent storm and shipwreck, recorded in Acts 27, might serve as an appropriate analogy for the church's present spiritual turbulence. I'd like to return to the analogy, because it precedes one of the most important questions that must be asked as God's people move toward the church of tomorrow.

At midnight, the sailors took soundings to determine the depth of the water. Knowing that they were nearing land, they dropped anchor and waited for daybreak. When the light of dawn allowed the passengers to physically see the land, they jumped into the water. Those who could swim made it to safety without assistance. Those who could not swim were instructed to float toward the land using broken boards from the ship, yet no one recognized the land to which they swam or floated.

Those who have been called out of the traditional church, should expect the same. The process of transfiguration will carry God's people to an unknown place of thinking, being, and doing. Christians should expect to see a change in the church's outward appearance as she prepares herself for her bridegroom. We would do well to help people trust God in the midst of this type of spiritual change.

While helping each other, one important question will naturally surface time and again: *if everything from the past ends up in the sea of yesterday, to what unknown land will people swim?*

This is the question that many souls are currently asking. Countless spiritual leaders would probably say that the question defines the church's present reality, because nearly everyone is *searching* for the answer!

The crew and passengers, who were forced to jump from a sinking ship, found their answer on the island of Malta. Their very lives depended on complete strangers! When they arrived, they discovered that the native inhabitants spoke an early Phoenician dialect and maintained a tribal society. Because of their language and culture, the islanders were thought to be barbarians, according to scholarship. In other words, they had not become *Roman-ized*. Nevertheless, the natives were friendly, hospitable, and kind-hearted. They welcomed the water-soaked swimmers with a warm fire for their comfort. In the end, much healing took place.

Likewise, the church of today must be open to a different way of communicating with people who don't speak *church-ese*. She must return to a simpler language and a more primitive way of living, thinking, and being, in the world. When the church realizes that her very life depends on the hospitality of complete strangers, she will meet the earth's inhabitants and find them to be—not barbaric—but friendly, kind-hearted, and eager to build a fire.

The church has always believed that *she* must save the *stranger* in his hour of need. But it's actually the other way around in the analogy of the shipwreck. If the ship represents the church, then the unknown islanders are the ones who save the church in *her* hour of need. Things often seem upside down when God turns things right-side-up.

I believe, therefore, that the unknown land, to which God's people must eventually swim, is a primitive approach to tribal survival—a *Net* of 144. This is the vision *Jesus* claimed for his bride, 2,000 years ago. It is the only way that the church will meet, and rely upon, complete strangers for her survival. In the end, I am convinced that much healing will take place.

I conclude, therefore, that the church must organize like a net, walk like a net, and talk like a net. Only time will tell if others will arrive at the same conclusion, as the wind of God's Spirit carries us into the church of tomorrow.

Acknowledgments

Many people stood by my side while the insights in this book were infused into my conscience and subsequently released to words. First, I'd like to acknowledge the encouragement of my husband, Larry. His enduring patience is beyond admirable. None of the research, or academic presentations that preceded this writing, would have been possible without his unwavering support.

I also wish to acknowledge my dear friend and spiritual mentor, Rev. Patricia Sibley, for her steadfast reinforcement during times when it could have been easy for her to dismiss my words, thoughts, and ideas. Her willingness to listen to my spiritual struggles during the four-year period of intense supernatural instruction, as well as the years that followed, helped me immensely.

I'd also like to thank Fran Kearns and Rev. Debbie Chase, for their editorial assistance, both technically and theologically. Their questions and concerns, over biblical accuracy and overall literary tone, enabled me to produce a better manuscript than I could have created without their guidance.

Bibliography

Levine, Amy-Jill; Brettler, Marc Zvi, ed. *The Jewish Annotated New Testament, New Revised Standard Version.* New York, NY. Oxford University Press, 2011

Brueggemann, Walter. *An Introduction to the Old Testament—The Canon and Christian Imagination.* Louisville, Kentucky: Westminster John Knox Press, 2003

Friedman, Richard Elliott. *The Bible with Sources Revealed.* New York, NY: Harper Collins, 2003

Barker, Kenneth, ed. *The NIV Study Bible.* Grand Rapids, Michigan: Zondervan, 1985

Kohlenberger III, John R. *The Interlinear NIV Hebrew-English Old Testament.* Grand Rapids, Michigan: Zondervan, 1979-1987

Kogan, Michael S. *Opening the Covenant: A Jewish Theology of Christianity.* New York, Oxford University Press, 2008

Mcknight, Scot; Rollins, Peter; Clark, Jason; Corcoran, Kevin. *Church in the Present Tense – A Candid Look at What's Emerging.* Grand Rapids, Michigan: Brazo Press, 2011

Bass, Diana Butler. *Christianity after Religion – The End of Church and the Birth of a New Spiritual Awakening.* New York, NY. Harper One, 2012

Meek, Esther Lightcap. *Loving to Know – Introducing Covenant Epistemology.* Eugene, Oregon: Cascade Books, 2011

Van Der Toorn, Karel. *Scribal Culture and the Making of the Hebrew Bible.* Cambridge, MA, London; Harvard University Press, 2007

Anderson, Herbert; Foley, Edward. *Mighty Stories, Dangerous Rituals.* San Francisco, California: Jossey-Bass, 1998

Tal, Duby: Haramati, Moni; Gibson, Shimon. *Flights into Biblical Archaeology.* Jerusalem, Israel, Albatross Aerial Photograph, Ltd. And Israel Antiquities Authority, 2007

Finkelstein, Israel and Silberman, Neil Asher. *The Bible Unearthed: Archaeology's New Vision of Ancient Israel and the Origin of Sacred Texts.* New York, Touchstone; a div. of Simon and Schuster, 2002

Scriptural Index

Prologue: Mark 9:3; Acts 27:27, 28; Acts 28:9; Mark 4:8; Luke 5:4; Luke 5:10b; Mark 1:18

1. Mark 6:33–44; Exodus 18:15, 17–21; Exodus 26, 1–6; Mark 6:7; Matthew 5:17–19

2. Mark 8:1–10; Mark 8:11–12; Mark 12:28–31; Deuteronomy 6:4; Leviticus 19:18; Revelation 21:15–17; Mark 8:8b

3. Mark 8:14–21; Mark 9:9; Mark 5:43

4. Luke 15:1–7; Luke 15:8–10; Luke 15:11–32

5. Mark 6:7; Matthew 10; Luke 9:1–5; Luke 10:1–23; Psalm 109:8; Revelation 21:15–17

6. Exodus 20:1–17; John 6:32, 33, 35a

7. Numbers 2:1–34; Numbers 1:21; Leviticus 24:5–9; Matthew 13:47

8. Acts 10:9–16; Acts 11:5–10; Acts 10:11, 34–35; Exodus 18:21; Revelation 21:1–2

9. Acts 20:7–12; Matthew 25:1–13

10. Matthew 13:47–49; John 21:1–6; Ezekiel 47:10

Epilogue: Revelation 21:2; Revelation 21:9; Exodus 18:21, 25; Mark 6:30–44; Luke 15:3–10; Mark 8:1–9; Acts 1:15; Acts 10 and 11; Revelation 7, 14, 21; Acts 27

About the Author

After twenty-two years of church ministry, as a director of music, art and theater, Ms. Wimmer sensed a strong call to remove herself from the institutional model of church organization. In 1995, she resigned from her leadership position and waited for direction. Shortly thereafter, from 1996 to 2000, Ms. Wimmer experienced an intense time of spiritual instruction. The inspired insights opened the door to fresh theological perspectives in three areas of human concern: Time, Language, and the Organization of God's people.

Believing that personal insight must be grounded in credible evidence, Ms. Wimmer entered the field of biblical research. From 2004 to 2009, she presented several academic papers at different regional and national meetings of the Society of Biblical Literature.

Ms. Wimmer believes that the kernels of wisdom, poured into her vessel many years ago, are intended to reorient the focus of the church of tomorrow. Therefore, she writes from a visionary perspective. She joyfully shares her inspired perceptions in an effort to sow seeds and contribute to the current dialogue in humanity's spiritual garden.

Ms. Wimmer lives in Tulsa, OK with her husband of forty-five years. In their free time, she and her husband enjoy gardening, carpentry, interior design, and renovating old or neglected houses. Together, they have two children and three grandchildren.